MAN'S PLACE

An Essay on Auden

MAN'S PLACE

An Essay on Auden

RICHARD JOHNSON

Cornell University Press

ITHACA AND LONDON

First published 1973 by Cornell University Press.
Published in the United Kingdom by Cornell University Press Ltd.,
2–4 Brook Street, London WIY IAA.

International Standard Book Number 0-8014-0764-8
Library of Congress Catalog Card Number 72-12406

Printed in the United States of America by Vail-Ballou Press, Inc.

Librarians: Library of Congress cataloging information appears on the last page of the book.

For Kay

Contents

Preface

In the most general terms, this book aims to show that the form and texture of Auden's poetry are best understood in the light of its underlying humanistic impulses. My focus is primarily on the specific ways in which the poetry works and on the particular challenges a modern humanism must face. To Auden, as to the Renaissance humanists, the means by which man expresses himself matters; the choice and use of words have both stylistic and ethical consequences. For this reason, much of the present study is devoted to scrutiny of the language of Auden's poems.

Auden is a philosophical poet, but in a manner that requires definition, especially since his beliefs have provoked much discussion. To Stephen Spender, "the truth of Auden's poetry rests partly in the fact that, however dazzling the effects, it offers at every point a paraphrasable prose meaning, and it can always be traced back to the system of ideas from which, in its different stages, it derives." Auden, says Spender, "is ultimately lucid and rational; but the surface of his work can be baffling." [1] This commentary, like so many on Auden's work, asks us to imagine poetry as something similar to Plato's cave:

1. Prefatory note to Herbert Greenberg, *Quest for the Necessary: W. H. Auden and the Dilemma of Divided Consciousness* (Cambridge: Harvard University Press, 1968).

the immediate surfaces—words, images, forms, sounds—are distorted shadows of more real, more lucid, more comprehensible ideas that exist somewhere behind that surface; behind these ideas, in turn, exist even clearer systems of thought. Understanding the poetry is conceived of as a process of getting through to those fundamental meanings.

Formulations like Spender's are misleading, particularly in view of the kinds of ideas that have been important to Auden's poetry, for Auden is a philosophical poet in a complex and paradoxical manner. The people mentioned in this study who have had the greatest effect on Auden have shared a deep respect for poetic exploration not simply as a means of saying but also as a primary mode of discovering and knowing. Martin Heidegger, whose influence on Auden is elusive but strong, is worth glancing at in this regard. Much of his work is directed toward exploring what he calls "preconceptual" knowledge. He argues that the history of philosophic thought has consisted of a progressive hardening of ancient ontological categories and a continuing neglect of the fundamental question of Being that the imposition of these categories originally obscured. He sees it as philosophy's task "to *destroy* the traditional content of ancient ontology until we arrive at those primordial experiences in which we achieved our first ways of determining the nature of Being." [2] For Heidegger, this means destroying the Cartesian dualism of consciousness and reality and exploring a more primary and unitary sense of what he calls Being-in-the-world. Moreover, Heidegger repeatedly insists that poetic language has on the whole been more successful in defining these primordial experiences than has philosophic language, which is itself based on a false ontology.

2. *Being and Time*, trans. John Macquarrie and Edward Robinson (New York: Harper & Brothers, 1962), p. 44; Heidegger's italics.

Hence, getting at the "system of ideas" behind Auden's work will, in this case at least, lead us full circle to the "baffling surfaces" of the poems (which, among other things, *are* both lucid and rational). We must deal with the language of the poems in order to be true to the philosophic systems, or rather predispositions, they reflect. Poetry here is the cohort of philosophy, not its servant.

The poems explore existence not by simple assertion or allusion, although they are full of both. Rather, they present models of existence that involve the reader in the process of exploration. The patterns of sound, imagery, syntax, rhyme, diction, metaphor, perspective, stanza, and argument are the means by which Auden assays his fundamental subject: man in the world. Even when Auden's language seems abstract, it is so partly in order to focus our attention on the relation between abstraction and experience as a prototype of man's status as both an experiencing and a reflective being.

The complexity of Auden's poems is a function of the complexity of his view of man. Auden develops complex poetic structures, on both the largest and smallest scales, to coordinate various aspects of man's being and to assess the nature of their relatedness. That he does so has two important consequences for the study of his poetry. First, the test of meaning in the poems is not the number of references to any given system of thought, but the way in which the poems treat the ideas they entertain; to approach the nature of man, Auden draws upon many sources, and modifies them as he uses them. Second, we must look at Auden's formalism as both a vehicle and a subject of exploration. In *Thanksgiving for a Habitat*, for example, the several poems about the various rooms of the house are grouped to indicate the relations among man's several activities and modes of being; the structure of the series is adjusted to reflect the structure of existence. Structure itself, because it is an aspect of being, becomes an object of inquiry; and what is said of structure in the largest sense applies equally to the smaller patterns of the poetry. The play of diction and syntax, and that of speaker, landscape, and view, are not simply techniques of presentation; they also create paradigms of existence. The arrangements, although formally gratifying in a way that should not be ignored, are also models of the order in which man exists, and need to be approached as such.

I have tried to create an organization that reflects the structure of Auden's longer works, where every part modifies and reflects every other. Chapters on a crisis in our sense of place and order, on perspective as an example of man's relation to externality, on varieties of poetic arrangement, on man's relation to nature, on action, and on man's capacity to fabricate a world are intended to supplement and modify one another. At the same time I have tried to avoid an organization so tight as to impede careful attention to individual works. Whenever a choice had to be made between organizational tidiness and full discussion of a poem, I have chosen the latter, partly on general principle and partly in response to the exploratory spirit that seems to me to dominate the poems.

My primary attention is to works written after 1940. This emphasis should not be taken to imply a specific theory of Auden's development, although I certainly disagree with those who see in the later poems a falling off from the accomplishments of the earlier ones. All the later works, and many of the earlier, seem to me parts of a single large enterprise, that of defining the uniquely human and of opposing those forces that have reduced our sense of our place in the world.

Permission to quote from the writings of W. H. Auden has been kindly granted by Random House, Inc., and Faber and Faber, Ltd. Portions of this manuscript first appeared in *The Virginia Quarterly Review*, Winter, 1972, and *The Yale Review*, Summer, 1972 (copyright Yale University); they are reprinted here, in altered form, by permission of the editors of those journals.

A fellowship from the National Endowment for the Humanities, supplemental grants from the Faculty Grants Committee of Mount Holyoke College, and a leave of absence from Mount Holyoke College enabled me to write this book. Arthur Mizener gave me steady portions of good cheer and a massive dose of special help when it was badly needed. LeGrace Benson, Stephen Ellenburg, Samuel Hynes, Kay Johnson, Ben L. Reid, and Jane Davidson Reid reacted and objected to parts or all of the various drafts of the manuscript. Helen Linda Dallas and Susan Moore Johnson discussed Auden with me during the course of their own work on him. Linda Young helped prepare the manuscript. To all I am grateful.

R. J.

London
February 1973

Bibliographical Note

Unless otherwise noted, I use titles and quote texts as they appear in *Collected Shorter Poems 1927–1957* and *Collected Longer Poems;* for more recent poems I use *About the House* and *City Without Walls*. Wherever possible, I also give a page reference to *Selected Poetry of W. H. Auden* (second edition), a handy and inexpensive volume. Unless date, place, or revisions of the original are important to my immediate purposes, I make no references to them. For detailed information on the history of the publication of poems and other works, the reader should consult B. C. Bloomfield, *W. H. Auden: A Bibliography: The Early Years through 1955* (Charlottesville: The University Press of Virginia, 1964), and Monroe K. Spears, *The Poetry of W. H. Auden: The Disenchanted Island* (New York: Oxford University Press, 1963). The primary texts of Auden's poetry and essays referred to, and my abbreviations for them, are:

ATH: About the House (New York: Random House, 1965)

CLP: Collected Longer Poems (New York: Random House, 1969)

CP: Collected Poetry of W. H. Auden (New York: Random House, 1945)

CSP: *Collected Shorter Poems 1927–1957* (New York: Random House, 1967)

CWW: *City Without Walls and Other Poems* (New York: Random House, 1970)

DH: *The Dyer's Hand and Other Essays* (New York: Random House, 1962)

EF: *The Enchafèd Flood, or, The Romantic Iconography of the Sea* (New York: Random House, 1950)

SP: *Selected Poetry of W. H. Auden,* 2d ed. (New York: Vintage Books, 1971)

SW: *Secondary Worlds* (New York: Random House, 1968)

MAN'S PLACE

An Essay on Auden

1. *Order*

Critics of Auden have, in general, either demanded too much intellectual consistency in his work or dismissed his ideas in favor of other principles of consistency. Such critical errors are understandable, for few poets of the modern age have so successfully created a poetry of ideas that is also a poetry of reality. One cannot ignore the discursive elements in Auden's poetry, or the keen intelligence working within the poems. At the same time, the ideas are modified and expanded by the poetic structures in which they exist, and these structures in turn are parts of a poetic world that is larger and more alive than the discursive statements from which it is made.

As a starting point for the attempt to explore and describe this world, we may put into general terms a few ideas that are basic to Auden's work of at least the last thirty years. All of them spring from the notion that man has an ethical need to know his place in the world.

Man is a double creature, aware of existing in two radically different spheres governed by radically different laws. "Necessity in my world," Auden says, "means two things, the givenness of whatever state of myself is at any moment present, and the obligatory freedom of my ego." [1] Man is an I and an it, an ego and a self, a consciousness as well as an object of

1. *Poets of the English Language*, ed. W. H. Auden and Norman Holmes Pearson (New York: Viking, 1950), II, xxvi.

consciousness. Moreover, when we talk of man's doubleness, we refer not simply to halves of personality but to something like the physicist's notion of complementarity; we refer to a basic paradox that exists in reality and is at the core of man's existence.

The world is also double, consisting of a natural world of iterative occurrences describable by natural laws, and a world of history, the world of unique persons interacting, in which no event is repeatable, and in which man can exist as shaper, creator, and agent.

Various forces in the modern era, including philosophical and scientific distrust of the existence of the outer world and of the reliability of the inner world, have confused and upset the balance between these spheres. Purely existential views of man that recognize only the freedom of the ego and deny the necessity of the self, as well as pseudoscientific definitions that treat the ego as if it were the self, create, in Auden's phrase, chimerical worlds; so also do the treatment of the world of history as if it were the world of nature and the treatment of the world of nature as if it were that of history.

The nature and role of art, it follows, are complex, but the play aspect of art is particularly important. Art, as a game of knowledge, focuses on both the similarities and the differences in the series of unities-in-tension which constitute man and his existence. Art as a formal order can image, though it cannot produce, the kind of order that men strive to create in their lives. Art as a made object celebrates man the maker of his own world. Art, because it both obeys laws of necessity and realizes freedom, can remind men of the existence of both. And art, playful art, debunks those heavens and hells of pure being that seduce men from their difficult but proper "purgatorial" course.

Auden's poetry and his criticism are filled with statements about man's place in the world, his relation to a total scheme of things. Although thoroughly modern in source and terminology, the statements are the product of a concern very similar to that which was once satisfied by the notion of man's privileged place in a great chain of being.

The phrase, "man's place," as I use it, refers also to the cumulative effect of Auden's celebration of Mother Earth: Dame Kind, as he often calls her. Man's place in this instance is expressed by a set of witty and complex figures for the biosphere, the physical place in which human life has evolved and, perilously, now exists. It refers to that place from which, in a twofold quest for an internal point of deep self-awareness and an external point of exact scientific observation, modern man has tried to escape. It represents the world conceived both as a dynamic and dangerous arena of experience and as the quotidian, prosaic locale of important moral acts. And yet the scientific understanding of the earth and the philosophical understanding of the world often take shape as the "Middle-Earth" of Tolkein, a familiar yet fanciful place whose resemblance to our world is clear if indirect.

I also use the phrase to signify the artificial world that man should and, often faultily, does construct as an expression of his humanness. Thus conceived, man's place is an arena of self-disclosure and action; it is the "world" as Hannah Arendt uses the term, a modern equivalent of the Greek polis and the Roman forum. In this sense, the figure has a political dimension, as a counterbalance to the otherworldliness and inner-worldliness that dominate the modern age.[2] I think these various senses of the phrase cover the ideas and images Auden

2. See *The Human Condition* (Garden City: Doubleday, 1959), esp. pp. 9–21 and 119–126.

means to indicate by the title of his recent work, *A Certain World*.

Each of these senses of the term leads ultimately to a concern with the use of language, the means by which Auden defines the human situation in its several significations. His poetic language has a multiplicity of qualities and functions: it is discursive, rhetorical, expressive, playful, and formal. It defines, discloses, and celebrates. It is fashioned into well-made poems. It is aesthetically pleasing and morally pertinent. Most important, when used properly, it is an instance of speech and thus a primary means of expressing that which is uniquely human.

To understand Auden's art we must recognize the reciprocity between his use of language and his ethical concern with the human position. Curiously, Auden's technical skill and his insistence that the poet is, above all else, a maker may have led critics to underestimate the forms he has fashioned. As much as these deserve praise as pure technical accomplishments, seeing them in simple technical terms does not do them full justice.

For Auden—perhaps for most poets—form is almost never simply a matter of craft. Auden, we may say, is a thoroughgoing gestaltist in the sense that he continually sees experience and existence in terms of pattern. Pattern is not just design imposed upon discrete experience; it is fundamentally more real than discrete particulars and atomistic sensations. Poetic form, then, is not just the artist's construction; rather, it expresses the fundamental stuff of existence: the relation between I and the world, between man's consciousness and his creatureliness, between basic integers of unity and multiplicity. Form, as a kind of oneness growing out of multiplicity, is the very essence of human existence, and is so treated by Auden.

We must therefore continually view form in connection with matters not generally thought of as being formal. The reciprocity between aesthetic ordering and order conceived philosophically goes both ways. If Auden's constructions cannot be understood except in a broad conceptual context, his concepts can be fully understood only as they "take form," that is, as they are manifested in poetic texture and structure. Auden's way of putting words together carries moral and philosophical weight, but it carries the burden lightly and in small packets. To understand his art and thought, we must follow with care his choice of words, his constructions of sentences, his control of voice, his assembling of images into landscapes, his making of metaphors, his choice and handling of meters and stanzas.

A useful starting point for this enterprise is *New Year Letter*, perhaps the first full articulation of the philosophical bases of Auden's mature style and, equally, a fine example of the way in which style details, refines, and clarifies meaning. The work is not a final statement of a systematic position. It advertises its own tentativeness by its epistolary form and its high-spirited, self-qualifying manner. It does not show much of the religious side of Auden, although its ideas are essentially those that underlay his formal return to Christianity. Nonetheless, because it is discursive in manner and eclectic in reference, it offers an introduction to ideas fundamental to Auden's later poetry and to some of his characteristic poetic tactics.

The poem's lively texture argues for a view of order as diversity-in-unity and against simple, static notions of order. It does so in part by the way in which it brings together an immense range of diverse references, discovering unity where one expects unrelatedness. The concords that Auden finds among physics, psychology, sociology, biology, literature, history, politics—the list is almost endless—exemplify the kind

of order of which he is talking. To say that the relation between the ego and the self or the perceiver and the world is
like that between particles and waves is not only a clever
figure but also part of a general proposition about the order
that exists in the world. Some of the best instances are in the
notes. For example, Auden juxtaposes James's description of
the growth of a "story" from a "germ" with an elaborate and
technical description of embryonic induction in the Triton
(a piece of tissue from one organism is transplanted to another,
resulting in growth according to the "inner logic" of the
transplanted tissue). This comparison comes as a note to a
general discussion of the similarities and differences between
art and life, and adds one more dimension to the comparison.

By its texture, allusions, and argument the poem makes the
point that the relatedness of things as seen by modern thought
is, for all the apparent diversity of approaches and subject, as
much an order (though one radically different in nature) as
that which allowed Pope to write *An Essay on Man*. This
yoking of past and present itself makes a point: the moral
problem at the root of the crises of our age grows in part from
the expectation that the same order men assumed in the past
can or should exist in the present. The poem's form embodies
a new view of the order of things, dramatizes the problem as
a conflict between *idées fixes* from the past (we "prefer our
idées fixes to be / True of a fixed reality") and the current
information we have, and finally asserts the necessity of our
knowing what kind of order we now exist in.

The overt occasion of *New Year Letter* is a coincidence of
events: the end of a year, the end of a decade, the end of
a historical era, and the beginning of the Second World War.
Its method is to approach the crisis defined by its occasion
from a number of different perspectives. The result is to as-

sert the multiplicity of the crisis and the necessity of a pluralistic view of it. As Herbert Greenberg has pointed out, the
three sections constitute a progressive enlargement of the historical context in which the crisis is viewed.[3] Part I of *New
Year Letter* talks about the year 1939; Part II about the 1930's
("Tonight a scrambling decade ends"); Part III about the
whole post-Renaissance epoch ("all the special tasks begun
/ By the Renaissance have been done"). This structure underscores a point made near the end of Part I:

> The situation of our time
> Surrounds us like a baffling crime. . . .
> And more and more we are aware,
> However miserable may be
> Our parish of immediacy,
> How small it is, how, far beyond,
> Ubiquitous within the bond
> Of an impoverishing sky,
> Vast spiritual disorders lie.   [*CLP*, p. 86]

So also, the poem spreads wide the investigation. It traces the
historical roots of the crisis; it brings to bear upon it a vast
collection of intellectual and artistic materials; it tries what
seems like every available perspective.

The crisis of the moment is primarily a crisis in man's
knowledge of himself and the world, and the immediate
problems—the dissolution of order in Europe and the rise of
fascism—stem from accepting simple solutions to complicated
problems. Thus, Hitler is someone with a dangerously simple
approach to a large philosophical tangle:

> Yet where the Force has been cut down
> To one inspector dressed in brown,

3. *Quest for the Necessary*, pp. 101–102.

He makes the murderer whom he pleases
And all investigation ceases.   [*CLP*, p. 86]

Like the Devil, as presented in Part II, Hitler personifies a brand of either-or thinking that everything in the poem's structure, texture, and argument opposes.

New Year Letter places an almost Augustan emphasis on man's need to know his place in a scheme of things; it does so through a spirited display of Augustan rhetoric. Part of the function of both the argument and the rhetoric is to suggest, by contrast, just how far we are from the kind of assumptions that served the Augustans. Both the need and the difficulty of meeting the need are summarized at the beginning of Part II:

How hard it is to set aside
Terror, concupiscence and pride,
Learn who and where and how we are,
The children of a modest star,
Frail, backward, clinging to the granite
Skirts of a sensible old planet,
Our placid and suburban nurse
In SITTER's swelling universe.   [*CLP*, pp. 89–90]

The expansion and contraction of metaphor mirror man's position as a finite creature in an infinite universe. As the domestic metaphor develops through homey, familiar language, the earth seems to shrink and the human presence on it to grow. Then, in the last line quoted, the terminology and the perspective shift suddenly: the familiar earth becomes a small and diminishing speck in an immense and growing universe. The way in which this shift is traced by changes in diction implies that part of what has made our sense of earth as home tenuous is the introduction of scientific perspectives.

This passage has to do not only with the substance and character of man's position but also with the intellectual equipment needed to "learn who and where and how we are," summarized by a neat aphorism that parallels the paradox of earth shrinking in an expanding universe:

> How hard to stretch imagination
> To live according to our station.   [*CLP*, p. 90]

Here, as in the passage quoted above, the couplet nicely holds together countermovements of expansion and contraction.

Next, the paradox is restated in terminology borrowed from gestalt psychology:

> For we are all insulted by
> The mere suggestion that we die
> Each moment and that each great I
> Is but a process in a process
> Within a field that never closes;
> As proper people find it strange
> That we are changed by what we change.   [*CLP*, p. 90]

The series of parallels and antitheses contrasts the vocabulary of common sense ("insulted," "mere suggestion," "proper people") with that of science. We think of ourselves as "proper people," whole individuals, and are told that we are merely a "process within a process." We are, the poem argues, both.

The paradox of man's nature and position, stated in terms attentive to what we know from modern astronomy, physics, and psychology, is in fact the central subject of *New Year Letter*. The order in which man can locate himself potentially exists, but it is a pattern of paradoxes and contradictions, not a simple linear order or chain. For Auden, the central paradox is that of man's double nature. By this Auden means that man knows himself as two radically different entities: as an existential I, the center of an anthropomorphic, egocentric universe that extends outward from each man; and as a physical me, an object, a small item in a giant universe that surrounds, includes, and acts upon him:

> There are two atlases: the one
> The public space where acts are done,
> In theory common to us all,
> Where we are needed and feel small . . .
> The other is the inner space
> Of private ownership, the place
> That each of us is forced to own,
> Like his own life from which it's grown. . . .
> Two worlds describing their rewards,
> That one in tangents, this in chords;
> Each lives in one, all in the other,
> Here all are kings, there each a brother.
>
> [*CLP*, pp. 111–112]

Again, the movement of parallels and antitheses is perfectly adapted to the topic, not only to the specific concern with the interplay of subject "I" and object "me" but also to Auden's general theme of "diversity-in-unity"; the dialectical movement of oppositions and syntheses is a rhetorical trope for our experiences of concord and disparity.

The very texture of *New Year Letter* argues man's doubleness:

> Hell is the being of the lie
> That we become if we deny
> The laws of consciousness and claim
> Becoming and Being are the same,
> Being in time, and man discrete
> In will, yet free and self-complete.   [*CLP*, p. 107]

The primary rhetorical technique here is antistasis.[4] By it, the poem indicates that even as we acknowledge doubleness, we must forsake both dualism and monism; not even the mechanics of verbal tense will allow them. The nature of man and of everything in the universe is "diversity-in-unity"; the pattern is one of "pluralistic interstices." Order is defined by our awareness of an intricate play of oppositions in which both oneness and difference exist; it must be conceived as a fruitful reciprocity between asymmetrical halves. Auden reiterates this point by means of a figure from modern physics:

> A particle, I must not yield
> To particles who claim the field,
> Nor trust the demagogue who raves,
> A quantum speaking for the waves.   [*CLP*, p. 109]

Each of the crucial terms refers to the nature and behavior of matter, specifically to the question of whether matter is ultimately particles or waves. By bringing together these terms Auden creates a verbal equivalent of the principle of complementarity, according to which light can be imagined only as being both quanta and waves: "an electron must sometimes be considered as a wave, and sometimes as a particle";[5] it is

4. "Repetition of a word in a different or contrary sense." Richard A. Lanham, *A Handlist of Rhetorical Terms* (Berkeley and Los Angeles: University of California Press, 1968), p. 11; hereafter, *Handlist*. I have tried to identify Auden's constructions and figures when this seems pertinent, not to suggest conscious adoption of schematized tropes but as a means of indicating the extent to which his art touches the most minute details of arrangement.

5. J. Robert Oppenheimer, *Science and the Common Understanding* (New York: Simon and Schuster, 1961), p. 69, as quoted by Norman Rabkin, *Shakespeare and the Common Understanding* (New York: Free Press, 1967), p. 22. Rabkin's discussion of the literary implica-

neither and it is both, and the inefficiency of our vocabulary, not the principle, makes it seem a contradiction in terms.

The scientific terminology is more than an ornamental diction. The principle of complementarity, like that of epistemological dualism,[6] reflects Auden's deepest awareness of the way things are. For all that he puts the notion of diversity-in-unity forward with a light touch—and at times, almost with braggadocio—he means it seriously. Man is both a Great I and a small speck; both an evolving animal and a Kierkegaardian Knight of the Infinite; both an observer and a part of the field he observes. Thus defined, his position is truly medial, but dialectically, not statically so. When Auden talks of man's being

tions is of interest, as is Frank Kermode's, in *The Sense of an Ending: Studies in the Theory of Fiction* (New York: Oxford University Press, 1968), pp. 59–64. To make my position clear: Kermode and Rabkin discuss the principle as a usable tool of literary criticism, with Kermode suggesting the limitations of using this kind of term too loosely; Auden, I am suggesting, uses it quite consciously as a figure of speech, one which also reflects a general attitude expressed in many other ways.

6. See note to line 447, in *New Year Letter* (London: Faber and Faber, 1941), pp. 101–102. Auden quotes Wolfgang Köhler's definition of epistemological dualism; see Köhler, *The Place of Value in a World of Facts* (New York: Mentor, 1966), 2d ed., p. 108. As I understand it, Köhler's argument is that the apparent conflict between the view that phenomena are "out there" and the view that "the genuine, the original, location of percepts must indeed be somewhere in our interior" (Köhler, p. 105) is the result of failing to distinguish between the phenomenal space, where "inside" and "outside" exist as relational words (whether between body and house or tree and house), and transphenomenal space, where the body is not a percept but an organism, in which certain neurological happenings called perception occur. All perception occurs within that organism's perceptual field, but "within" in this case doesn't mean the same as when applied to a house. We are, then, both perceiving organisms and perceived entities. This notion is one of the bases of the poem's language and argument.

a particle in a field, a process within a process, he is being both literal and metaphorical. Indeed, one of the distinctive features of all his metaphorical language is that it generally arises from literal description.

Analysis, word play, and allusion work in harness. The fourth paragraph of Part I, for example, opens with a deceptively simple set of antitheses:

> To set in order—that's the task
> Both Eros and Apollo ask;
> For Art and Life agree in this
> That each intends a synthesis.   [*CLP*, pp. 80–81]

Both the agreement and the diversity of Eros and Apollo are figured by the chiasmus of the second and third lines quoted, an effect complicated by the treatment of the personifications as synonyms: we readily identify Apollo with Art; the identification of Eros with Life is less simple. The antithetical terms are united by "agree in this," an agreement underscored by the rhyming word "synthesis." That the point of agreement of the antithetical forces is "that each intends a synthesis," coupled with the chiasmus, creates a four-line diagram of diversity-in-unity. Agreement and disagreement are both the subject and the poetic method.

Matters become both more complicated and more unified when order is defined. The syntax and diction create a patterned interplay of oneness and diversity that both explains and exemplifies order as

> The symmetry disorders reach
> When both are equal each to each,
> Yet in intention all are one,
> Intending that their wills be done
> Within a peace where all desires

> Find each in each what each requires,
> A true *Gestalt* where indiscrete
> Perceptions and extensions meet.   [*CLP*, p. 81]

Again, part of the effect comes from discussing similarities and differences between art and life in a series of parallel statements about the way in which each attempts to bring particulars into wholeness. Thus, "in intention all are one" has a double meaning: art and life strive toward the same thing and all things move toward oneness. Again, the scientific diction is instrument as well as ornament. The allusion to the gestaltists, who emphasize the organized quality of perceived objects and the continuity of the field of perception, makes a tight metaphor for order among apparently discordant objects. In such an order the discreteness of phenomena disappears both in theory (gestaltists do not recognize the discreteness of objects) and in fact (a true gestalt is one in which there is no division of phenomenal extension and perceptual activity). Diversity in oneness is made tactile by the compressed and orderly lines of logic and syntax and, also, by the submerged metaphor, underscored by the rhyme, that develops from the pun on "indiscrete" and suggests an illicit rendezvous.

The statements in *New Year Letter* about the nature of art are fully consistent with the metaphysical positions it assumes. At the end of Part I the poem argues that language, precisely because it has the qualities of indirection and contradiction, has a crucial function:

> So, hidden in his hocus-pocus,
> There lies the gift of double focus,
> That magic lamp which looks so dull
> And utterly impractical
> Yet, if Aladdin use it right,
> Can be a sesame to light.   [*CLP*, p. 104]

Double focus is gained by the use of verbal mechanisms that, for instance, will show human nature as composed of simultaneously and radically contradictory aspects. The case is one of complements, not supplements. Man is "I" and "me" at once, and, strictly speaking, his totality is not the sum of both, but rather the simultaneous fact of both, just as the two aspects of matter are contradictory in ordinary discourse but not in mathematical formulae. Poetry has for man the function of a higher calculus by which it is reasonable to see man as a totality, even though he is composed of contradictory and antagonistic elements.

The poem begins by asserting that man cannot act properly until he has stretched his imagination to know his proper place, but this is only a temporary suspension, and not an evasion, of the question of action. In view of the complex nature of things, action based on false presuppositions about the world—action, for instance, that counters the lie of intellectual hegemony by committing itself to emotional hegemony—is very likely to produce the opposite of what it intends. But, once the nature of man's position is grasped, action is, though difficult, a proper response of earthbound man to his medial position:

> . . . we're free to will
> Ourselves to Purgatory still,
> Consenting parties to our lives,
> To love them like attractive wives
> Whom we adore but do not trust,
> We cannot love without their lust.   [CLP, p. 107]

Freedom, then, is not merely, as for Engels, the recognition of necessity, though it is that in part. It is also the recognition that we "live in time," the recognition of the temptation, given the anxiety that living in time produces, to try to escape that anxiety by embracing an illusory absolute (like "perfect freedom"), and the choice to accept existence in time. This choice is put in the familiar terms of landscape and journey, Auden's most persistent figures for "here" and "now":

> Time is the life with which we live
> At least three quarters of our time,
> The purgatorial hill we climb,
> Where any skyline we attain
> Reveals a higher ridge again.
> Yet since, however much we grumble,
> However painfully we stumble,
> Such mountaineering all the same
> Is, it would seem, the only game
> At which we show a natural skill . . .   [*CLP*, p. 108]

This passage suggests a commitment to earth that comes from our awareness of the dangers of commitment to anything else. Indeed, the images of landscape and earth throughout the poem accumulate into a kind of gravitational reinforcement of the suggestion that we must both find our place and recommit ourselves to act within the proper sphere of our existence. Exact formulations for action are either make-believe heavens or deceptive hells. In between the unreachable and the undesirable is a middle, normal, purgatorial state, with normality defined as a series of in-betweens, of interstices, as motion and journey. And this view points to a playful, self-mocking art that nonetheless aims at clarification and action, based on an order in which

> . . . Freedom dwells because it must,
> Necessity because it can,
> And men confederate in Man.   [*CLP*, p. 127]

The paradoxes of necessary freedom and permissible necessity are the contingencies upon which man's confederation with other men rests. It is fashionable to see Auden as someone who has avoided entangling commitments to action by playing elaborate poetic games; the poem indicates something quite different. Man must act. In one sense, he acts all the time. But unless he is properly aware of the possible ill consequences of his action they are likely to occur; the poetic games are a means of gaining this awareness.

As an epistle in closed couplets, *New Year Letter* often echoes the great Augustan discursive poems. The form immediately calls our attention to the question of order and to the difference between our present crisis and that system of order whose fall is partly the cause of our present crisis. The particular kind of patterning that marks the Augustan epistle —a constant interplay of parallels and antitheses, based especially on witty conjunctions of words and word senses— becomes in Auden's hands an especially useful tool for presenting and discussing complex ideas of order; the form domesticates the sophisticated arguments on which it is based. And the collocation of a whole range of intellectual references for what seem at first to be metaphorical purposes produces a sense of congruity among the various systems of knowledge alluded to.

Auden has not made exclusive use of the closed couplet in an extended work since *New Year Letter*, which succeeds, when it does, largely because of the couplet. Diversity-in-unity should be considered the poem's most important theme, and it is one for which the couplet, with its contrasts and antitheses, is a very suitable vehicle; formally, the couplet *is* a constant interplay of oneness and multiplicity. Subsequently, the poet's increasingly complicated view of man's place and nature demands a greater variety of forms than is afforded by the long epistle of couplets. Much of the interest that works written since *New Year Letter* hold comes from the new forms Auden has found or created to accommodate this developing view.

2. *Perspectives*

Seeing things clearly, "as they are," is a root value in Auden's poetry; it is also, the poems suggest, a difficult task. A great many of the poems, early and late, offer the mechanics of perception and the consequences of viewing something from a given perspective as a metaphor for the action of disentangling illusion from reality; this, Auden suggests, is a primary function of the moral imagination. But, although the artistic effects never lose their ethical edge, they develop into something larger than their original cause. Seeing clearly is one of Auden's richest themes: not just a technique, a stratagem, or an injunction, but a fundamental human action and goal that deserves and receives full poetic exploration and articulation.

That Auden's earliest poetry strives for a clinical, diagnostic detachment is a commonplace.[1] The stance seems to be derived from several sources: from Auden's youthful scientific interests, from a reaction against the sentimentality of Georgian verse, from the Hulme-Eliot aesthetic ascendant during Auden's undergraduate years, from the analytical methods of psychoanalysis, from the scientism of Marxist socialism, and, perhaps as the artistic integer of these various impulses, from Hardy: "What I valued most in Hardy, then, as I still do, was his hawk's vision, his way of looking at life from a very great

1. See Spears, *Auden,* pp. 6–10.

height, as in the stage directions of *The Dynasts*, or in the opening chapter of *The Return of the Native*." [2] This specific image appears in "Consider," one of the finest of the many early poems that give specific instructions for viewing:

> Consider this and in our time
> As the hawk sees it or the helmeted airman:
> The clouds rift suddenly—look there
> At cigarette-end smouldering on a border
> At the first garden party of the year.
> Pass on, admire the view of the massif
> Through plate-glass windows of the Sport Hotel.
>
> [*CSP*, p. 49]

2. *Southern Review*, 6 (1940), quoted by John Fuller, *A Reader's Guide to W. H. Auden* (New York: Farrar, Straus & Giroux, 1970), p. 47. Fuller also sees a source of the hawk image in Lawrence's *Fantasia of the Unconscious* (1922), p. 62. For an interesting recent commentary on this poem and on John Fuller's analysis of it—especially of the image of the "supreme Antagonist" in stanza two—see Roy Fuller, "The filthy aunt and the anonymous seabird," *Times Literary Supplement*, 21 May 1970, pp. 561–562. John Fuller says that "critics take the 'supreme Antagonist' to be death, but the tautology implicit in death making the highborn mining captains 'wish to die' seems clumsy" (p. 47). Roy Fuller accepts the view of this "subsequent commentator" over his own original view that the antagonist is death. J. Fuller bases his view on a notebook entry (BM Notebook, Fol. 44) that identifies Satan as "the Censor, responsible for repressing man's natural instincts and bringing about that self-consciousness which separates him from the rest of the animal kingdom." But thence to call the antagonist Satan seems invalid. Surely, Auden is talking about the death wish (which Freud defines as the wish of the unconscious to return to an earlier stage of evolution, where there is no consciousness), wittily thought of as Satan, rather than the other way around. It is tautological to say that the death wish, personified as Death, would make us wish to die—escape consciousness and the anxiety it carries with it—but the tautology is to the point.

Hawks and airmen suggest sharp sight, remoteness, mobility, and danger; they also have heraldic and heroic associations, the hawk through the rituals of falconry, the airman as the only really glamorous fighter of the First World War, who alone was free of the trenches, free to engage in single combat. Together the two viewers, fusing the animal with the human, the medieval with the modern, and the natural with the mechanical, define seeing clearly as a complex discipline, achieved only by great effort.

What makes "Consider" interesting and instructive is, first, the things its perspective reveals. Those who attend garden parties, wear furs, and go to places like the Sport Hotel are both "ruined"—infected by the universal death wish that permeates any decadent society—and incapable of recognizing that they are. The smouldering cigarette-end is a portent, a kind of fuse; the furs and the window are vain attempts to ward off an invisible "polar peril," a new ice age. One needs the sharp sight, detachment, and cruelty of the hawk and airman because the symptoms are covert, because those now under the microscope delude themselves so easily, clothe themselves in such illusions as those "supplied . . . by an efficient band." The encroaching disaster is within range of vision; its symptoms are strongly felt, as, for instance, they "make the farmer brutal / In the infected sinus." But only the truly sharp-sighted will understand these symptoms as the antic forms of the universal death wish. The point of view, then, is one that not only allows us to "see" more but also makes possible the correct diagnosis of such apparently harmless signs as a cigarette-end or

   . . . silted harbours, derelict works,
   In strangled orchards, and a silent comb

Where dogs have worried or a bird was shot.

[*CSP*, p. 49]

The physical perspective is a way of describing the kind of intellectual perspective needed to interpret a difficult set of symptoms. Our tendency to clothe ourselves in illusion requires that we seek detachment, coldness, and even cruelty; the goal here is psychological and sociological, as well as physical, realism. The view has its roots in Freud as well as in Marx: what Freud saw as the death wish corresponds to what Marx saw as the inevitable decay of the bourgeoisie.

Despite the poem's apparent orthodoxy of argument, critics both early and late have found it possible to applaud it without attending to its argument. In a discussion of the poem first published in 1939, Cleanth Brooks finds that the accommodation in a dramatic unity of warring elements is "Auden's best certification as a first-rate poet though it will hardly recommend him to propagandists of one sort or another, or to proponents of an immediate cause. . . . The proponent of the cause will prefer to the complexity of drama with its real conflicts the knocking over of a straw man." [3] Brooks is careful to note that he grants Auden the right to have serious political views, but the clear implication is that the politics of the poem must ultimately be at odds with the richness of its irony.

John Bayley goes further. He suggests that "Consider" is effective *because* it is at odds with itself: "The poem's calm and detached tone contrasts remarkably with the fever and dread it describes. As so often, Auden is describing present-day society as if it were seen by a schizophrenic, indeed as a schizophrenic would see any society and any of life's phe-

3. *Modern Poetry and the Tradition* (Chapel Hill: University of North Carolina Press, 1939), p. 133.

nomena." The crucial word here is "any," for if this perspective would show any society and any phenomenon in the same way, what is revealed has no value as specific diagnosis. Auden, Bayley argues, is a propagandist luckily manqué; because "Auden identifies himself with both sides, with the doomed order and with the forces of progress," [4] and because his almost Dickensian vision triumphs over his conceptual diagnosis, he is saved from the heavy-handedness of socialist realism and propaganda art.

Brooks and Bayley both assume the ideological content of a poem to be a probable impediment to its aesthetic success. Both use a simple argument: dogma is simplistic and unresponsive to the complexities of life; art is complex and responsive to the ambiguities and complexities of experience; hence the two are at odds, and a good poem will inevitably move away from dogma. Bayley goes so far as to suggest that, if necessary, a good poet's artistic sense will rebel, on its own, against the poet's doctrinaire leanings.

What Brooks calls a structure of dramatic ironies and what Bayley sees as a romanticist, or schizophrenic, sensibility in Auden is, I think, actually the fruit of a highly developed comic sense, which is naturally skeptical of dogma qua dogma —it is indeed the most effective way of attacking the dogmaticness of dogma—but not necessarily antagonistic to social criticism of the sort that this poem so clearly makes. Brooks and Bayley are both talking about something that is in the poem, but they are talking about it in such a way as to discount or disregard other things that are also in the poem. The whole poem, I think, rests on a comic disproportion between a carefully inflated and hyperbolic rhetoric—what Monroe Spears calls "clinical Baroque"—and a "scientific" analysis of

4. *The Romantic Survival* (London: Constable, 1957), pp. 160, 161.

social and individual ills. Neither element cancels the other.

There is, of course, good reason for associating detached observation with the comic mode; what needs to be emphasized is that, even in what is generally thought of as a rather doctrinaire poem, Auden's detachment is that of the comic observer as well as the clinician; in fact, the clinical distance is achieved in part by comic technique. And this helps account for the irreverence toward dogma found here as elsewhere in Auden. "Consider" is not antagonistic to its own diagnoses; rather, the comic method gives them a different coloration.

The details chosen to describe both the condemned way of life and the destructive force, although they portend disaster, are also the source of a comic exuberance far from morbid; their portrayal comes close to caricature. In this sense, Bayley seems to me correct; there is a real involvement in the quotidian details of life that makes the poem more than a piece of propaganda. But the vision is not schizoid, for, being basically comic, it can both ridicule and enjoy, empathize and analyze, with only that sense of strain integral to any comic art. Ian Watt, in *The Rise of the Novel*, describes *Tristram Shandy* as offering formal solutions that provide "a way of reconciling Richardson's realism of presentation with Fielding's realism of assessment"; [5] this seems to me an apt description of what Auden achieves in this poem. He maintains both a sense of life and an analytical perspective; and the means by which he does so is verbal play.

The style of "Consider" is thoroughly and intentionally indecorous, especially if thought of as a diagnostic report. The last stanza taunts in a magnificent grand hortatory manner:

5. *The Rise of the Novel: Studies in Defoe, Richardson, and Fielding* (Berkeley: University of California Press, 1959), pp. 290–291.

Seekers after happiness, all who follow
The convolutions of your simple wish,
It is later than you think; nearer that day
Far other than that distant afternoon
Amid rustle of frocks and stamping feet
They gave the prizes to the ruined boys.   [*CSP*, p. 50]

The use of a highly rhetorical style to describe the trivia of "ruined lives" is meant to be risible; the mode is primarily mock-heroic, and the manner and the message qualify, but do not disqualify, each other. But the heightened style serves also to suggest that seeing things clearly, thus understood, is in its own way heroic. In terms of the imagery, the world of those who fool themselves is a trivial world, characterized by frocks and school festivities; that of those who face reality, even destructive reality, has the grandeur of glaciers, of "the great northern whale." Ceasing to delude oneself has at least the advantage of enlarging the universal fight against death; it transforms a battle against "neurotic dread" into one against a Supreme Antagonist.

The basic system of values is Auden's special mélange of Marx, Freud, and others; it also seems to me cognate with that of Bergson. Bergson sees as comedy's largest function the correction by laughter of those mechanized gestures that impede freedom and evolution. What this poem finally does is to show the symptoms of social and individual illness as mechanized, automatic, sclerotic gestures, and by its treatment of them to prompt the freedom—ultimately, the freedom to evolve—that comes from laughter. Both the vision and the technique are comic. The stylistic gamesmanship, the social and moral seriousness, and the comic irreverence are in harmony.

Seeing things clearly, "facing reality," remains a major value in "Consider"; the perspective one must adopt to do so, however, is broader and more complicated than the term "clinical" suggests. The goal of the perspective is what Auden calls, in "Through the Looking-Glass," the untransfigured scene: reality—social, historical, psychic, biological—not only confronted directly, but also defrocked of illusion so that the viewer can participate in it. Unlike other poets—Wordsworth or Wallace Stevens—who celebrate the naked encounter of the imagination and reality, Auden does so only partly for the experience itself. The major goals are knowledge, leading to action, and disenchantment, leading away from other actions. We should have no illusions about reality, because illusions restrict freedom. In another sense, they are part of reality, in a way that a comic perspective can nicely show; the point is that we need to know that illusions *are* illusions. Behind this view lies the assumption of something like a normative moral reality. For Stevens, to use an obvious contrast, each of the thirteen ways of looking at the blackbird constitutes a way of knowing a part of reality; at the same time, each way partly falsifies, by being incomplete, and even when taken in toto they do not give absolute knowledge of the blackbird's reality. Auden argues the necessity of a complex perspective, but he sees it as a means by which one can know reality, albeit a different kind of reality from that Stevens is concerned with.

This is not to suggest that Auden ignores either the richness or the importance of the encounter between man and reality. In "On This Island," for example, he reverses the traditional romanticist formulation of the encounter and, at the same time, suggests and demonstrates the importance and fecundity of the reversed exchange:

> Look, stranger, on this island now
> The leaping light for your delight discovers,
> Stand stable here

And silent be,
That through the channels of the ear
May wander like a river
The swaying sound of the sea.

[*CSP*, p. 82; *SP*, pp. 20–21]

"On This Island" is, in several ways, a quite remarkable tour de force. By the instructions he gives, the speaker makes the viewer almost totally passive, while attributing to nature the "shaping powers" Coleridge finds in the human imagination. In the opening lines, "the leaping light," not the stranger, discovers the delights of the scene. The figure used to describe the viewer's perception is intricate. Terminology associated with the external view (channels, river) is applied with anatomical and conceptual precision to the perceiver, so that both he and the perceiving organs are coordinated with the external world. The figure of speech pulls the perceiver into the world he perceives; and the ear, a passive and nondistorting sense organ, receives attention equal to that given the eye. At the same time a covert metaphor comparing viewer to island (both have channels and rivers) is developed, with the implication that the same kinds of productive interactions that occur between island and ocean can also occur between the small, isolated, passive viewer and the large, inchoate world about him.

At the heart of the poem is a comparison that can be expressed as follows: mind is to reality as island is to ocean. The two spatial coordinates—mind-reality and island-ocean—parallel each other in a complicated fashion. The ear, for example, has both literal and metaphorical channels; the field, in stanza two, "ends," while the viewer "pauses" (the gerund "ending" and the imperative "pause" are so placed as to underscore, by momentary grammatical confusion, this comparison); the harbour is like memory; and the full view is like clouds. Our relation to externality, these comparisons suggest, is like that of land to water, with a junction between at which it is difficult to distinguish them. Acts of perception become figures for man's general relation to the world, for his place.

The intricacy with which figure and image interact in this poem itself becomes a trope for the drama presented. Auden uses the literal images from the description of island and ocean to represent the interaction of mind and reality. That is, perceived images stand as figures for the act of perceiving; the images represent the act by which they are perceived. When we arrive at the final figure, which compares the full view entering memory to the clouds passing the harbour mirror, we are aware that the "full view" includes the island, the ocean, the cliffs, the ships, the clouds, and the harbour, things that have represented both seer and seen. In a variation on synecdoche, the viewer's view is represented by parts of that view, and the act of perception is projected into one more dimension.

There are further complications within the figure. By the parallel construction the clouds passing the harbour mirror are implicitly compared to the ships going out to sea, which in turn are compared to seeds, an image that brings us back to the land. Moreover, the harbour—a part of the ocean, partly enclosed by the island—is a mirror, making water an analogue for mind, elsewhere represented as land. Memory stretches back in time, in contrast to clouds that, mirrored, "through the water saunter"—thus stretching, implicitly, into the future. This comparison introduces time into what have been spatial comparisons and immediately complicates the time comparison by making the mirror images move, appropirately, in opposite directions. The central image of harbour mirror in a sense doubles the poem, makes us watch the sea and island expand both outward (from harbour) and inward (through memory). The whole poem is constructed as a series of metaphors for the interaction of mind and actuality—with a movement away from the perceiving mind towards externality—of which this is the last: it dramatizes the act of establishing external reality as an expansive rather than a reductive process.

A further source of the power of "On This Island" is its translation of images and figures into what Father Walter Ong has called the "aural correlative." Auden recalls that "when in 1935, I first tried to read Marianne Moore's poems, I simply could not make head or tail of them," because, he goes on to note, of the syllabic verse, "in which accents and feet are ignored and only the number of syllables count." (*DH*, pp. 296, 297). This poem, first published at the end of 1935, is almost surely his attempt to come to terms with Miss Moore's syllabic stanzas,[6] a remarkable achievement for someone first encountering this difficult form. (Auden doesn't quite keep the syllable count from stanza to stanza, and he seems at times

6. According to John Blair, Auden "had followed Marianne Moore into syllable-counting verse"; see *The Poetic Art of W. H. Auden* (Princeton: Princeton University Press, 1965), p. 150 n. 50. Blair argues, correctly, for an early date for Auden's experiments with syllabic verse, and I think this an even earlier instance. "Casino" (CSP, p. 97), which also first appeared in *Look, Stranger!* (1936), is an early example of the use of the Horatian ode, which, along with Miss Moore's syllabic stanzas, is the major source of Auden's syllabic verse. John Fuller, in *Reader's Guide*, p. 176, argues for the Freud elegy as Auden's first poem in syllabic verse. Because the use of the form is important in the development of Auden's humanism, the matter of dating is of some importance; 1935 seems to me worth considering as the beginning of Auden's serious interest in the form as used both by Horace and by Miss Moore.

close to an accentual-alliterative meter.) One effect of the form is to emphasize the "thingness" of the words, hence to make the words interact "metrically" quite as the images they denote interact physically. As emphasized by repetitions and alliterations, and by the many internal rhymes and partial rhymes, the individual words become units that act upon one another much as the individual images in the poem interact, as, for example, in "When the chalk wall falls to the foam and its tall ledges / Oppose the pluck / And knock of the tide," or in "Diverge on urgent voluntary errands." Given our account of the ways in which image and figure work in the poem, this formal arrangement of sounds means that the metaphors take on a visual and aural shape. The formal and aural arrangements of the terms for perception create new coordinates parallel to those already described.

The opening instructions for viewing are comparable to those in "Consider"; they seem, in fact, almost the same formula: Consider/Look; this/this island; in our time/now; hawk-helmeted airman/stranger. Both poems define a manner of viewing, an object, a time, and a viewer. The words "this" and "now" are the crucial words of the first line, even of the whole poem; by them, Auden emphasizes the importance of the present time and place. In effect, he says: all these delights will follow if only you will look at, or be receptive to, things here and now, not there and then. In light of this we may take "stranger" to mean not visitor but the figurative stranger, the estranged, the inhabitant who has ignored this time and this place, and must therefore reacquaint himself with reality. "For us like any other fugitive," he writes in "Another Time," "It is to-day in which we live."

Even as Auden discounts the notion of the imagination as the creator of reality, he projects the encounter between man and the external world as a full and lively exchange, and makes the exchange reverberate in the figuration and versification of the poem. Indeed, the poem strongly implies that the less man imposes his special stamp on reality, the more delightful as well as the more enlightening his exchanges with it will be. Thus the moral and the aesthetic work together in productive economy; the poem itself seems to be on an urgent, voluntary errand, in which duty and delight are fully coordinate.

"On This Island" seems to me both an implicit attack on the misshaping powers of the imagination and a brilliant celebration of the productivity of normative, restrained perception. The poem has the air of a careful logical demonstration that perception which attempts to clarify can also bear poetic fruit. We must, it seems to say, see reality clearly if we are to act wisely, but we do not necessarily impoverish reality by doing so; sense and sensibility have, in fact, common sources.

Auden uses the mechanics of perception as a basic structural principle primarily to assert the moral value of seeing clearly, separating illusion from reality, using the imagination to work through overlays of false constructions. Héctor Agosti, in trying to construct a defense of art that is compatible with Marxism, puts the case for this kind of realism as follows:

When it has freed itself from the idealistic illusion that it is creative in itself, consciousness becomes really creative. It is not a cosmic and personalized consciousness, but one that is intimately personal and human, immersed in things, which throws light on the individual and social interplay of thought and act.[7]

Auden's artistic contributions to these supraartistic goals are at least three. First, he recognizes that much of the problem concerning such crucial matters as action, reality, community,

7. "A Defense of Realism," in *Documents of Literary Realism,* ed. and trans. George J. Becker (Princeton: Princeton University Press, 1963), p. 501.

love, freedom, and, most of all, humanity is really lexical, the result of a careless use of words crucial to our understanding of these matters, and he sets poetry the task of clarifying their meanings. Second, he sees the creation of a poem as a crypto-political act, by which every poem is "very nearly a Utopia," where the ideal human conditions of love, freedom, and community exist. And third, he sees the playful actions of poetry as a means of freeing consciousness of illusions concerning its own creativity and hence allowing consciousness to become truly creative.

Auden's image for this last function of art is the mirror; his most famous statement of his preference for mirror art appears in the opening paragraphs of his review of T. S. Eliot's edition of Kipling's verse:

Art, as the late Professor R. G. Collingwood pointed out, is not Magic, i.e., a means by which the artist communicates or arouses his feelings in others, but a mirror in which they may become conscious of what their own feelings really are: its proper effect, in fact, is disenchanting.

By significant details it shows us that our present state is neither as virtuous nor as secure as we thought, and by the lucid pattern into which it unifies these details, its assertion that order is *possible*, it faces us with the command to make it *actual*.[8]

Long before Auden used the critical figure of speech "mirror art" he used the mirror as a poetic image. And if "mirror art" sounds like a fairly simple tag, an image of naive realism, Auden's realism is in fact far from simple, either conceptually or in practice.

Probably the fullest early treatment of the theme and use of the image come in "Through the Looking-Glass" (*CSP*,

8. "Poet of the Encirclement," rev. of *A Choice of Kipling's Verse, New Republic*, 109 (24 Oct. 1943), 56. Auden's italics.

p. 74), first published in 1933.[9] The poem is in many ways interesting and powerful, in some ways cumbersome. Most interesting is its statement of the interdependence between approaches to reality and kinds of love. The poem attempts to connect a movement from illusion to clarity with one from selfish to selfless love. The world of illusion and selfish love is presented as a distorted image, probably in the glass covering a portrait; Auden attempts, without complete success, to fuse the images of a distorting mirror and a work of art (the portrait):

> There move the enormous comics, drawn from life—
> My father as an Airedale and a gardener,
> My mother chasing letters with a knife.   [*CSP*, p. 75]

"Drawn" has two meanings, sketched and removed. One kind of seeing has the tendency to take people out of life, and distorts them; this is a distortion that we associate with "art." The contrasting image comes in the last stanza:

> With you enjoy the untransfigured scene,
> My father down the garden in his gaiters,
> My mother at her bureau writing letters . . .

> [*CSP*, p. 76]

The means of getting from the former view to the latter seems to be surrender to a Laurentian life force, an act of sensual acceptance. But the poem, to my mind, is dealing with more material than its form can handle. Indeed, it is not really until *The Sea and the Mirror* that the images and the themes they represent receive full artistic expression and exploration, a fact that suggests just how rich the themes are.

9. The various revisions of the poem, especially of the first stanza, are of interest, because they show Auden attempting to establish exactly the "right" perspective.

The title, which was added for the 1945 *Collected Poetry*, suggests the direction in which Auden had been moving since the early 1930's. When Alice walked through the looking glass, she found a world that was in some visual ways and some metaphorical ways the mirror image of the world she left behind. In the same spirit, Auden's means of achieving clarification is often comic reversal.[10] The well-known ballad "As I Walked Out One Evening" (*CSP*, p. 85; *SP*, p. 24) goes much further than "Through the Looking-Glass" in making the mirror of comic art serve the interdependent goals of clarification, love, and action. The poem's structure makes artificial simplicity and simple artificiality throw light on each other.[11] It works in much the same way as a medieval animal débat: we cannot judge the truth of any of the statements uttered by our general sense of how likely it is for any of the speakers to be using a particular kind of speech.

10. Auden knows a good deal about how mirrors and mirror images work. For an instructive example, see Martin Gardner, *The Ambidextrous Universe: Left, Right, and the Fall of Parity* (New York: Mentor, 1969), p. 120: "Wystan H. Auden, a great admirer of the Alice books, raises a similar question in his poem *The Age of Anxiety*. A right-handed Irishman, sitting at a New York bar and contemplating his reflection in a mirror says:

My deuce, my double, my dear image,
. . . What flavor has
That liquor you lift with your left hand . . . ?

Liquor contains grain alcohol, which . . . has a symmetrical molecule. Like the water in milk, it, too, would be unaffected by mirror reversal. But liquor also contains carbon compounds called *esters* which give it flavor, and most esters are asymmetrical. No one knows what flavor Looking-glass liquor might have, but it is a good bet that it would not taste the same as ordinary liquor; unless, of course it were tasted by a Looking-glass Irishman."

11. See Cleanth Brooks and Robert Penn Warren, *Understanding Poetry*, 3d ed. (New York: Holt, Rinehart and Winston, 1960), p. 333.

Problems of interpretation arise if we treat the poem as we would a dramatic monologue or any other form of poetry in which the veracity of a dramatized speaker is at issue.[12] Indeed, one of the things the poem does is to play games with such expectations. In the end, we accept the message of the clocks, not because we find them more reliable than the lover or the original speaker, but because we have been led carefully through the arguments of the various conventionalized voices to accept the clocks' imperatives. The poem is based on a ventriloquism to which readers of ballads should be well accustomed: someone makes a general argument by speaking at different points in different voices.

When Brooks and Warren note that the lover "voices the lover's universal claim to an eternal love, but . . . in a tired and sleazy idiom," [13] they are slightly incorrect. The singer of the song is doing an imitation of a lover using hyperbolic imagery, or, to go back a step further, a sophisticated poet is writing a folk song in which the singer imitates a lover spouting comically bad poetry that is, however, generally in the idiom of the folk song; both the lover's language and the comic hyperbole are characteristic of the idiom. The point is important because each of these frames within which we see or hear statements involves a shift of our perspective on those statements (as well as being the source of the kind of wit that, for instance, has a clock saying "let not Time deceive you").

Probably the best description of what happens in a poem like "As I Walked Out One Evening" is Auden's own characterization of poetry as a game: a serious game, a game of knowledge and discovery, but still a game. Much more than "Through the Looking-Glass," this poem relies on the play

12. See, for example, Ellsworth Mason, *The Explicator*, 12 (1954), Item 43.

13. *Understanding Poetry*, p. 333.

of perspective as a means of moving from illusion to reality to commitment. This is a far "simpler" poem than the earlier one, but its simplicity is achieved and contrived, a mature simplicity. There is, as the clocks deliver their speech, a careful progression, one that works, however, within the bounds of the adopted convention:

> 'In headaches and in worry
>   Vaguely life leaks away,
> And Time will have his fancy
>   To-morrow or to-day.
>
> 'Into many a green valley
>   Drifts the appalling snow;
> Time breaks the threaded dances
>   And the diver's brilliant bow.
>
> 'O plunge your hands in water,
>   Plunge them in up to the wrist;
> Stare, stare in the basin
>   And wonder what you've missed.'
>
> [*CSP*, p. 86; *SP*, pp. 25–26]

Remembering that the controlling images in the poem all have to do with water and that these stanzas are being "chimed" by "all the clocks in the city," we can see how the careful and subtle play of perspective becomes the instrument of discovery. The image of water, which suggests both fullness (in the original reference, "brimming river") and temporal flux ("the deep river ran on" in the last), here takes such witty forms as "vaguely life leaks away" and, with its pun, "appalling snow." Dances are threaded in the sense that dancers seem to be controlled by strings. "Broken strings" as an image for the destructiveness of time is remarkably compressed, and the compression continues with the second object of "Time breaks." The diver's brilliant bow is, presumably, the arc of his dive; the arc is broken when the diver hits the water, so along with the general sense of time rendering aging divers incapable of performing with brilliance, there is also the basic sense that a dive is ended because it occurs in time. Thus the speaker is making the clocks, in their "grim reaper" tone, view time as potentiality, which is not so far from that view implicit in the image of the "brimming river," and is also the basis for the injunction to commitment and love. The play of images continues when the diver's bow is immediately followed by the injunction to " 'plunge your hands in water.' " The argument is trickier than it looks, because, having described time conventionally as destructive, the clocks then advocate another immersion, as if to say that our fulfillment as well as our destruction lies in time.

The injunction to stare in the basin begins the metamorphosis of the image of water from one of time to one of awareness. The images of the desert and the glacier suggest again that full awareness means an acceptance of the potentiality of time; an avoidance of temporal flux results in sterility—lack of water—or glacial freeze. The naiveté and the sophistication of the speakers play against each other to manipulate the reader's responses. As a result, when the final injunctions to look come in the last three stanzas, the voice of the poem, here ventriloquized as the clocks—but arguing a point rather different from their original grim message—has taken on a carefully achieved authority. It comes not because we suspend our awareness that this is a poet's use of a folk-song idiom but because we are aware of just how wittily and well he is using it. Artifice does not camouflage itself; quite the contrary, it calls attention to its artificiality.

In the crucial stanzas, then, we accept the instructions to look at ourselves and the world because the poet has earned the right for his ventriloquism to be heard. Far from being lulled into a state of simple acceptance, we are teased into a state of complex awareness about degrees and kinds of simplicity, extravagance, and artificiality. The kind of simplicity that exists in these stanzas differs markedly from what we might call a primary folk song:

> 'O look, look in the mirror,
>   O look in your distress;
> Life remains a blessing
>   Although you cannot bless.

> 'O stand, stand at the window
>   As the tears scald and start;
> You shall love your crooked neighbour
>   With your crooked heart.'   [*CSP*, p. 86; *SP*, p. 26]

The series of imperatives comes as a logical development: plunge, stare, wonder, stand at the window, love. Each act leads to the next. We are first enjoined to enter into reality, then to look, first in the basin, then in the mirror, then through the window; that is, to move from illusion through awareness of self to awareness of what is outside the self. Then, on the basis of the clarified scene, we are told to love, not romantically, but, as it were, biblically.

Using the basic materials that appear in "Through the Looking-Glass," this poem achieves its success not because Auden has found a way of wittily presenting a serious point of view, but because he embeds a serious moral statement in a complex play of perspectives that leads the reader to the point of earning the "simple" moral statement. It leads us through a series of exercises in discernment, in seeing, so that the reader knows what it means to make moral statements of substance. The whole poem involves the reader's participation in turning conventions around, finding that images change their meaning in different contexts, testing statements by re-phrasing them. This is exactly what Auden means when talk-ing abstractly about poetry as a game of knowledge.

The continual redefining of relations between work of art and reader or viewer is both subject and tactic of one of the finest of Auden's poems, "Musée des Beaux Arts" (*CSP*, p. 123; *SP*, p. 49). The poem's celebration of art—the kind of art Brueghel exemplifies and Auden achieves—is based on the notion that by bringing a viewer into its own complex world, art can free him so that he may freshly confront reality, un-hampered by "artistic" delusions that extract experience from context. By taking the viewer into "another time," this anach-ronistic art can convince him that "another time has other lives to live," that "it is to-day in which we live" ("Another Time," *CSP*, p. 170; *SP*, p. 65). The ultimate effect of the poem is an "awareness of being *with* time, i.e., experiencing time as an eternal present to which past and future refer," [14] an experience on which action can be based. By bringing us into the timeless world of art, the poet forces us back into time.

What seem to have struck Auden about Brueghel's "Land-scape with Fall of Icarus" [15] are the multiple incongruities of style and subject and the ways in which these are focused to present a scheme of values. All that is seen of Icarus, in the

14. Auden, Introduction to *The Living Thoughts of Kierkegaard* (Bloomington: Indiana University Press, 1963), p. 7.

15. See F. Grossmann, ed., *Brueghel: The Paintings, Complete Edition,* 2d ed. (London: Phaidon, 1966), Plate 3a. Plate 3 reproduces the version in the D. M. van Buuren Collection, which differs most notably in the presence of Daedalus hovering above the scene.

version of the painting in the Musées Royaux des Beaux-Arts in Brussels, is a faint leg disappearing into the water. Dominating the painting are a ploughman and his horse, a shepherd and his sheep, a large ship, painted in the minutest detail, a busy port and several other ships. Except for that scarcely visible leg, it is a contemporary landscape, painted with all the homely realism that we expect of Brueghel.

As Max Bluestone has pointed out,[16] this is not the only Brueghel referred to in the poem (nor, for that matter, are all the examples necessarily Brueghels). The first stanza brings together references to paintings of several kinds of "extraordinary" events: "suffering," "the miraculous birth," "the dreadful martyrdom," each of which is treated by the old masters contextually, in its human position. We may, taking this into account, read the poem as a bitterly ironic condemnation of man's indifference to suffering, and see Auden reading Brueghel as condemning those who go on with their business while "real" suffering occurs about them. On this basis we would read the first lines—"About suffering they were never wrong, / The Old Masters: how well they understood / Its human position"—to mean, the old masters understood that men usually ignore the suffering of others.

This reading seems to me only partially correct. Auden lauds Brueghel not only for his realism about human indifference, but even more for his compositional imagination. In all the paintings referred to in the poem, the events we usually think of as extraordinary—birth, massacre, martyrdom, death—are placed in a context of ordinariness, so as to make the viewer break down his customary distinctions between the extraordinary and the quotidian:

16. "The Iconographic Sources of Auden's 'Musée des Beaux Arts,'" *Modern Language Notes*, 76 (1961), 331–336.

Evil is unspectacular and always human,
And shares our bed and eats at our own table,
And we are introduced to Goodness every day.

["Herman Melville," *CSP*, p. 145]

Through the anachronisms and the witty style, Brueghel, according to Auden's reading, works to erase divisions between the mythic and the prosaic, the past and the present, the spectacular and the ordinary. We are made aware, simultaneously, of the banality of Evil and the reality of evil. Brueghel engages us in the art of seeing the details of daily life because, according to Auden, that is where suffering as well as miracles occurs. If we think of the Icarus story as an allegory, Icarus can be seen as the figure of the aesthete who uses his art to try to escape the world of immediacy, of homely things, who, despite all the interesting and ethically demanding things around him, chose to try to approach the sun, and ended, pictorially, as a quick stroke of the brush.

The poem's power derives in part from its tone, almost the verbal equivalent of Breughel's manner. The way in which Auden maintains a conversational, low-keyed, ~~prosy~~ manner and still argues a difficult point is at the heart of the poem's distinction. Through this tone Auden treats the Brueghel paintings with as superb a combination of loving care and nonchalance as Brueghel treats his subjects. Equally important is the way in which an implied situation recasts the poem's "argument" onto a cognate dramatic plane. The title places the speaker not simply in front of the paintings but in a museum. (To make the title a matter of major importance in the poem is surely justifiable, because it is only through the title of Brueghel's painting that we really know its "subject": we would be unlikely to think of the painting as being about Icarus on the basis of one leg sticking out of the water.) By calling attention to the speaker's location, the title suggests an analogy between the museum and its paintings, on the one hand, and the world outside on the other. The Brueghel painting argues for awareness of the ordinariness of the miraculously good and the miraculously bad. It suggests a continuation of its own complex sense of anachronistic relatedness to the world outside the museum, not simply Brussels in 1939, since the relation would exist to any time, any place.[17] The same applies to the poem before the reader; we should react to it as it reacts to the Brueghels.

Perspectives on various kinds of reality and on various artistic representations of reality are shifted so as to inculcate in the reader a sense of his own relation to reality. As the reader is led from Auden to Brueghel to Icarus to the events in the Christ story, and from Brussels in 1939 to sixteenth-century Flanders, he gains an awareness of the extension of all of these events into his own time and place. The events referred to in the first stanza of the poem—the Christ story—are not as peripheral as the poem's offhand manner might imply. Auden insinuates the continuity not only of events in general but specifically of the events of the birth and martyrdom of Christ. The suggestion is made so deftly that one wants not to overstate the case. But Auden is ultimately suggesting, without labeling it, a Christian awareness of time as he, following Kierkegaard, understands it: "time is neither conquered nor escaped, but possessed."

The aesthetic mechanism, then, works not simply as an effective way of presenting a message, but as an essential tool for understanding experience. In his "Preface to Kierkegaard," Auden says that

17. It seems to me, however, worth reading as a companion piece to this poem "Brussels in Winter," *CSP*, p. 123.

Kierkegaard is a dangerous author, because the more he attracts, the more he has the opposite effect to the one he intends, which is to throw the reader back upon his own experience. To become a disciple of Kierkegaard is to betray him, for what he would teach is an approach to oneself, not a conclusion, but a style of questioning to apply to all one's experience, including that of reading him.[18]

This states a basic assumption of Auden's art. The relationships that the poems establish between themselves and the reader function not as subtle didacticism but as essential methodology, as a discipline of knowing; the perspective shifts constantly to put the reader into the position of being able to see. Thus, multiple and shifting perspectives are not only a technique but also a way of involving the reader's reactions so that they become a part of the poem's being. All poetry, of course, plots to affect its readers, but Auden's strategy is so to tease the reader with shifts of diction and syntax and vantage point as to involve him in a definable way in the processes of the poem.

To understand perspective in its fullest sense, then, we are led to questions concerning the status of the poem vis-à-vis both its maker and the reader. Moving the reader about by shifting perspectives is a way of making him aware of his "human position." This positioning occurs not only in those poems where perspective is specifically identified, but also and continually through the interplay of words, phrases, and metaphors.

In "Whither?" (*CSP*, p. 119), which has the function of establishing the perspective for the entire volume *Journey to a War*, literal shifts in perspective and subtler shifts in word order create a sensation, appropriate to the poem's title, like

18. *New Republic*, 110 (15 May 1944), 686.

that of the traditional description of a man looking through the window of a moving train, uncertain if it is he, the ground, or the train that is moving:

> Where does this journey look which the watcher upon the
>   quay,
> Standing under his evil star, so bitterly envies,
> As the mountains swim away with slow calm strokes
> And the gulls abandon their vow? Does it promise a juster life?

The first sentence moves us through a series of vantage points. The journey "looks"; the "watcher" (his position triangulated by two prepositions, upon and under) is by name a point of perspective, and he is watching the movement not simply of the boat but of the abstract journey; someone, implicitly, is watching both the journey and the watcher; the mountains move "with slow calm strokes," giving us the sense of the movement of both mountains and boats and of the relative status of the one movement to the other; the gulls follow the boat but "abandon their vow," which is, presumably, the vow to follow the ships all the way out to sea—again, both the gulls' and the general watcher's perspectives are implied. The only movement not explicitly stated—but continually implied —is that of the boat, the "actual" movement that is taking place. But this is just the point. All of these movements *are* relative, in the Einsteinian sense, not figuratively but really. Every movement away from is a movement toward; movement always depends on perspective and on relative motion. And the second short question of the stanza translates the physical perspective into moral terms: the "juster life" becomes, for all its simplicity of phrasing, as much a matter of multiple perspective as the physical journey.

Auden is not toying with perspective: he is using it to ask

crucial questions. Is the journey as relative morally as it is physically? Is there, somewhere in all this relative movement, a fixed point and an actual direction? The answer to the first question is positive: "His journey is false, his unreal excitement really an illness / On a false island where the heart cannot act and will not suffer." But, again through a complex discipline of shifting perspective, the possibility of its being a "true journey," one in which real movement occurs, is discerned:

> But at moments, as when real dolphins with leap and panache
> Cajole for recognition or, far away, a real island
> Gets up to catch his eye, his trance is broken: he remembers
> Times and places where he was well; he believes in joy,

> That, maybe, his fever shall find a cure, the true journey an
>   end.   [*CSP*, p. 119]

The poem "Whither?" achieves its goal by moving the reader through physical uncertainty to possible certainty, expressed in the same manner as the uncertainty of the first lines; the uncertainty begins to become a principle of certainty; the leap and panache of the dolphins, the island that appears to get up to catch the viewer's eye, remind the viewer of constants within the field of motion. The commitment to journey becomes an acceptance of the constancy of relative motion, like the "purgatorial hill" and "penitential way" in *New Year Letter*.

The Sea and the Mirror describes and enacts the processes by which a multiple perspective creates a complex realism. It is an example and a defense of comic play as a means of knowing, defining, and celebrating man's problematical nature and condition. It begins by allowing Prospero to applaud himself for his renunciation of art and his freeing of Ariel; it proceeds by exploring the ramifications of this act; it ends by endorsing and celebrating art, properly used, not to alter or create, but to comprehend reality and man's place in it. Its art makes us aware of the limitations of art.

The work has been quite properly praised for the felicity of its formal arrangement:

Tautly organized, its components balance and interweave with one another. The pleasure to be had from the whole supplements, in the Coleridgean sense, the pleasure to be had from its parts. The Stage Manager's short prologue parallels Ariel's brief epilogue spoken to Caliban; Caliban's earthy but involuted prose address to the audience complements Prospero's dignified and colloquial address to Ariel; and the short speeches of the other characters collected under "The Supporting Cast, Sotto Voce" are enclosed in the center of the poem. These people form not only the pivot of psychological interest but are centrally located so as to seem accessible to the influences acting upon them from outside, notably those of Prospero, Ariel, and Caliban.[19]

Edward Callan, among others, has illustrated in detail the intricacy of its design. The whole "is arranged like a triptych with separate panels for the artist, the work of art, and the audience"; Part II is

an elaborate pageant like Prospero's wedding masque in *The Tempest*. All the characters in *The Tempest* except Prospero, Ariel, and Caliban appear here as personified types; and each speaks in an appropriate verse form. . . . There is first the suggestion of a circle—the symbol of the macrocosm, and of perfection. Within

19. Frederick P. W. McDowell, "The Sea and the Mirror," in *Auden: A Collection of Critical Essays*, ed. Monroe K. Spears (Englewood Cliffs: Prentice Hall, 1964), p. 142.

it "courtly" and "low" characters alternate. . . . The arrangement of the characters also suggests a social order, as Alonzo holds the central position and the courtly and rustic characters are proportioned on either side of him between the lovers.[20]

The work has a ceremonial, processional quality, with characters, forms, and ideas paired off in intricate balances, giving the reader the pleasure of finding the achieved design.

It is, moreover, an allegorical arrangement. Auden's diagram for the work, preserved in his notebooks, indicates some of the correspondences: [21]

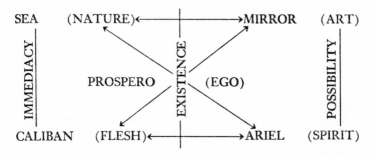

The characters correspond in part to psychological entities, with Prospero representing ego and poised between Caliban (the flesh) and Ariel (the spirit); in part to ontological categories, with existence poised between immediacy and possibility; in part to more general philosophical categories, with spirit and flesh poised against each other; in part, to aesthetic categories, with characters representing the relation of art to nature. There is, further, a whole set of congruencies between

20. "Auden's Ironic Masquerade: Criticism as Morality Play," *University of Toronto Quarterly*, 35 (1966), 136.

21. Lockwood Library MS, p. 105. Reproduced in Spears, *Auden*, p. 247. Reprinted here by permission of W. H. Auden and The Poetry Collection of the Lockwood Memorial Library, State University of New York at Buffalo.

Auden's work and *The Tempest*, so that we are aware at all times of both Shakespeare's characters and Auden's recreation of them.

In Auden's essay on the relation between Master and Servant, part of which is devoted to *The Tempest*, he makes the following proposition: "To present artistically a human personality in its full depth, its inner dialectic, its self-disclosure and self-concealment, through the medium of a single character is almost impossible" (*DH*, p. 110). One solution to this dilemma is to dramatize an inner dialectic as a relationship between two or more characters. In particular, Auden sees the master-servant relation as a dramatization of the dialogue between the ego and the self. His reading of *The Tempest* is based on the notion that it is in part an allegory of the "inner dialectic" of the human personality. *The Sea and the Mirror* presents both this reading and its own allegory of human character.

If it is an allegory, however, it is not a simple one. Prospero, for example, has several references: the ego as viewed by Shakespeare (as read by Auden), the ego as viewed by Auden, existence as understood by each, and the artist as viewed by each. There is, moreover, some evidence that Auden disagrees with Shakespeare on crucial matters and that he is presenting that disagreement in the work: "*The Tempest* seems to me a manichean work, not because it shows the relation of Nature to Spirit as one of conflict and hostility, which in fallen man it is, but because it puts the blame for this upon Nature and makes the Spirit innocent" (*DH*, p. 130). We must, then, avoid an oversimplified view of either the design or the message of *The Sea and the Mirror*. For all its formal congruencies, and partly because these are so highly elaborated, the structure is not static. For all that it is diagrammatic in its conception, it is exploratory and analytical in its execution. It constantly examines its own form and raises the question of what is real and what is contrived. Auden's properly acclaimed skills as an arranger, a formalist, and an epigrammatist are fully manifest, but taking the work as a whole, we end with an awareness not of schematized compartments and emblematic characters but of the ironic resonances among them. Just as the center of the original diagram is the point at which the various forces converge on "ego"—that is, consciousness—so the whole works progressively toward transforming general consciousness into specific awareness.

The status of the work as a critical commentary is the source of a whole extra and complementary set of staging and role-playing situations, themselves complicated by the fact that Shakespeare was so conscious of stagecraft and so often used stage metaphors; the continual teasing is in the best Shakespearean spirit. Talking of Prospero's masque in *The Tempest*, E. M. W. Tillyard remarks: "On the actual stage the masque is executed by players pretending to be spirits, pretending to be real actors, pretending to be supposed goddesses and rustics." [22] And in reference to Prospero's ensuing speech ("such stuff as dreams are made of"), S. L. Bethell notes,

The final organisation of Shakespeare's experience is thus functionally related to the dual consciousness of play-world and real world, characteristic of Elizabethan playhouse psychology. If Shakespeare put the whole of life into his plays, he reciprocally interpreted life in terms of the theatre.[23]

22. *Shakespeare's Last Plays* (London: Chatto and Windus, 1938), p. 80.
23. *Shakespeare and the Popular Dramatic Tradition* (London: Staples, 1944), p. 41.

Auden's work, then, at once underscores and multiplies the multiconsciousness of Shakespeare's work. For instance, Auden implicitly, by the arrangement of the Supporting Cast, gives his version of Shakespeare's Prospero the opportunity to create a wedding masque, to rearrange the characters for a second time. But Auden then uses his version of Antonio to comment on the "resolution" that each of these characters, under the influence of Prospero, has reached. Auden compounds our awareness of the artificiality of art by showing the characters as Shakespeare's creations, manipulated by Prospero, but, in the instance of Antonio, incompletely manipulated. The "real" characters of Auden's piece are artificial reconstructions of the "real" characters of Shakespeare, and we are made aware of the artificiality of both sets of "real" characters. In another sense, the artificial characters are the reality. We are made aware that there are no "real" personages "behind" the created ones. The reality of the stage is its artifice.

All of this is magnified and restated in Caliban's long address to the audience. Caliban, Auden's recreation of Shakespeare's creation, stands in front of the curtain—in the "real world," or halfway between it and the stage world—and in the "role" of Shakespeare addresses the audience, itself a fictional creation. He takes on the role of the audience, then switches back to the role of Shakespeare, then plays the role of Shakespeare playing the role of the young artist who, at one point, looks in the mirror and sees: Caliban. As has often been noted, he does so using a style that echoes James's prefaces to the New York edition and equally—and more revealingly, perhaps—both the style and the logic of that most teasingly artificial dramatist, Oscar Wilde. In the midst of all this artifice and role-playing, Caliban uses himself as the representation of reality and becomes the spokesman for the "real" human condition, part of which, however, is that we are all "born actors," that we always retain our "incorrigible staginess." Not only the style of Caliban's speech but also its sentiment seems Wildean. Life imitates art, in a sense, and art imitates life inasmuch as we are all stagy.

"Who we really are" is what Caliban finally represents, which helps to explain why Auden gives him the long final speech and makes him the role-player par excellence. That is, if we interpret Auden's parenthetical designation of Caliban as "Flesh" (in the diagram) in the light of his comment that Flesh means "the whole physical-historical nature of fallen man" (*DH*, p. 131), he is "who we really are": conscious egos conscious of a self. And the reason for using Caliban as the representative of this self is clear. Since we think of Shakespeare's Caliban as being grotesque and subhuman, that "monstrous wreck," his role shocks us into awareness of our unwillingness to recognize our existence as historical-physical beings. Thus it is Caliban who, as the "subject" of art, answers the audience's call for the author, and Caliban who stares the young artist in the face when that artist looks his imagination, his Ariel, in the eye and sees his own reflection:

Striding up to Him in fury, you glare into His unblinking eyes and stop dead, transfixed with horror at seeing reflected there, not what you had always expected to see, a conqueror smiling at a conqueror, both promising mountains and marvels, but a gibbering fist-clenched creature with which you are all too unfamiliar, for this is the first time indeed that you have met the only subject that you have, who is not a dream amenable to magic but the all too solid flesh you must acknowledge as your own; at last you have come face to face with me, and are appalled to learn how far I am from being, in any sense, your dish; how completely lacking in that poise and calm and all-forgiving because all-understanding good nature which to the critical eye is so wonderfully and domestically present on every page of your published inventions.   [*CLP*, p. 237; *SP*, pp. 99–100]

What confronts us in "Caliban to the Audience" is a corporate image: the self, forever playing roles, observed by an audience, which he himself represents, undertaking the task of self-recognition. In this light, the audience comes to represent our own awareness, or lack of awareness, of our self. Our self is what our cognitive ego recognizes as our being. It is not a zonal concept, not a compartment of personality; it is our awareness of ourself as a third as well as a first person. It is not just the body, the physical organism, because, from the inside, we are not immediately aware of ourself as a body—the body is a concept, not an experience. Perhaps the best term is that which Auden uses along the tangent from Caliban (flesh) to Sea (nature) in his diagram: immediacy. Though "immediacy" applies to external as well as internal sensations, we are not, in our most basic form of awareness, cognizant of the difference between internal and external nature: this is a distinction made by a "higher" mode of thought.

Prospero represents awareness, recognition, volition: our consciousness of ourselves as conscious beings who can be, but do not like to be, aware of a self. For Auden, *The Tempest* is in part a parable of the result of the Fall, and of the ensuing unwillingness of the ego to accept the self: not the unwillingness to accept the absolute demands of the self, but to accept that we have a self, an unattractive and demanding creature like Caliban. Prospero, having tried to master and improve the self, commits the manichean heresy of trying to disinherit him; and the self, like Groddeck's It, keeps reminding the ego that it is always there. If Prospero the artist represents the ego, then the work's various statements about art are also statements about the nature, functions, and duties of the ego in relation to the self, just as the statements about Prospero's rulership are also statements about the rulership of the self by the ego. The work does not cease to be a parable of the nature, functions, and responsibilities of the artist *per se;* the several planes of the allegory continually reflect each other. The production of artifacts serves as a means of dramatizing the general human propensity to try to work magic with the self, and it is ultimately with the human impulse, not the cultural products, that Auden is concerned. In fact, artistic creation is viewed in part as a healthy sublimation of the impulse to try to be a magician with human life. Auden, then, is not talking simply about the limitations of poetry. He is also talking about the limitations of an artful mentality, and about the degree to which the ego can or should attempt to govern the self. In the end, Auden celebrates a kind of art, like that of *The Tempest,* that can disillusion us about the power of artfulness and urge us back into the "real" world where art has only a limited use.

As an allegorical figure, Prospero is avoiding his true responsibility, both in his effort to control completely by his art and in his attempt to free himself from any responsibility, to become only a spectator, the cognitive but not the volitional ego. The exact nature of his responsibility is difficult to define. In "Balaam and His Ass," Auden talks of the volitional ego as a servant in relation to both the superego and the self, each of "whom" is a master "who is either obeyed or disobeyed"; it is a master only in relation to the body, which "can never be a master, nor even a servant, [but] only a slave" (*DH*, p. 112). These definitions would appear to leave little area of responsibility for the ego. In "The Virgin & The

Dynamo," however, he talks of "the ego's consciousness of itself as striving-towards, as desiring to transform the self, to realize its potentialities" (*DH*, pp. 65–66). Although it cannot be master of either the superego or the self, the ego exercises a directional power by choosing whether or not to obey or disobey either: "I act towards my states of being, not towards the stimuli which provoked them; *my* action, in fact, is the giving or withholding of permission to myself to act" (*DH*, p. 172; Auden's italics).

The ego can, moreover, abjure the will to complete power or complete autonomy. Some remarks from "Squares and Oblongs" are useful here. St. Augustine, Auden says,

was the first real psychologist for he was the first to see the basic fact about human nature, namely that Natural Man hates Nature. . . . His ego resents every desire of his natural self . . . because desires are given not chosen, and his ego seeks constantly to assert its autonomy by doing something the requiredness of which is not given . . . a pure act of choice.[24]

To satisfy this desire, he engages in one of two kinds of *actes gratuites:* crime, which is magic, "an attempt to make free with necessities," or innocent games, one instance of which is art.

In *The Sea and the Mirror* art can be understood as either kind of gratuitousness. On the island, Prospero attempts magic, over other people and over himself. After his renunciation, he "frees" Ariel, presumably to allow him to play innocent games. In "Balaam and His Ass" Auden has this to say about Ariel:

Imagination is beyond good *and* evil. Without imagination I remain an innocent animal, unable to become anything but what

24. *Poets at Work*, ed. Charles D. Abbot (New York: Harcourt Brace, 1948), pp. 167–168.

I already am. In order to become what I should become, therefore, I have to put my imagination to work, and limit its playful
activity to imagining those possibilities which, for me, are both
permissible and real. . . . But, once imagination has done its work
for me, to the degree that, with its help, I have become what I
should become, imagination has a right to demand its freedom to
play without any limitations, for there is no longer any danger
that I shall take its play seriously. Hence the relation between
Prospero and Ariel is contractual, and, at the end of the drama,
Ariel is released.   [*DH*, pp. 133–134; Auden's italics]

Has Prospero, when he frees Ariel, become what he should? I
think Auden, in his rendering of the story, shows the limitations of Shakespeare's Prospero and "corrects" him, making
him recognize the limitations of Ariel's play and making him
free Ariel when Ariel has done his "work." But it is difficult
to say whether or not Prospero has "become what he should
become" because there is, as such, no plot to the work.

The well-ordered middle section, however, can be taken
as an indication of the effects of Prospero's artistry, although
its order must be evaluated in the light of the larger order of
the whole work. Although we cannot really distinguish between Auden's hand and Prospero's in the arrangement of
Part II, I would argue that Auden presents the wedding
masque as a positive instance of art actualizing the possible in
a proper, untyrannic fashion. Each character realizes his own,
not an arbitrarily chosen, nature. The bond uniting each character to himself is a form of love. And the whole "circle" is
both satisfying and imperfect. Freedom and necessity interact,
and the image of the wedding governs everything and everyone. The whole web of harmonious relations within the
poems, between each poem and the character who speaks it,
and among the various forms and characters is aesthetically

satisfying in a way that does not suggest improper interference with life. Art seems to be performing its proper function.

Antonio, as several critics have pointed out, is the test case. According to Callan, "Antonio represents the typical romantic hero—Faust, Don Juan, Captain Ahab—whose solitary end is despair." Blair, accepting this view, sees Antonio's lines—"while I stand outside / Your circle, the will to charm is still there"—as a sign that there will continue to be temptations to Prospero "once more to use his magical art, even though he has now outgrown his Romantic trust in the imagination as a substitute for life." [25] According to Justin Replogle,

Antonio's message is, nothing is right, or, rather, nothing has changed. If for God, everything that is is right; for man everything is wrong. Antonio plays the role of devil or genuine knight of faith. The two are mirror images, one almost perfectly good, the other almost perfectly evil. . . . Prospero's image, shriveled as it is beneath Antonio's fastidious scorn, shrivels only to life size from its formerly too-large dimensions.[26]

It is difficult to construct a character out of Antonio's words, and surely there is too little evidence on which to base an interpretation like that of Callan and Blair. But Antonio, in his choric commentaries on each of the resolutions achieved by the "minor" characters, is the proof that Prospero has used his art as a wise ruler and not as a tyrant, and Antonio, in an odd sort of way, has also come to a kind of resolution with his own nature. As Frank Kermode, using Auden's lines to support a point he is making about Shakespeare's Antonio, puts it,

25. Callan, *Toronto Quarterly*, 35, 139; Blair, *Poetic Art*, pp. 114–115.

26. *Auden's Poetry* (Seattle: University of Washington Press, 1969), pp. 74–75.

"A world without Antonio is a world without freedom; Prospero's shipwreck cannot restore him if he desires not to be restored, to life. The gods chalk out a tragicomic way, but enforce only disaster. The rest is voluntary." [27] Auden's Antonio, too, is the proof that the resolutions achieved are the work of the beneficent use of art, not of magic transformation. He is, to use Caliban's words, the "unforeseen mishap" that intervenes to ruin the dramatist's effect "without, however, obliterating . . . the expectation . . . that there was an effect to ruin" (*CLP*, p. 248; *SP*, p. 111). By challenging each of the resolutions achieved by the other characters, he demonstrates that these have the proper tentativeness.

Each of Antonio's rejoinders takes the form of an assertion of the independent "I." Antonio does not represent the Romantic hero or the principle of evil, and certainly not the genuine knight of faith; rather, he represents a principle of sheer ego, which denies the existence of the self and of other people; that he is a usurper reinforces his image as unfettered ego. But more important is his role in defining negatively what Prospero can do and has done: "All by myself," he says, "I tempted Antonio into treason." On the evidence of *The Tempest*, Prospero's temptation of Antonio takes the negative form of failing to rule; he forsakes his role as ruler in favor of his books and magic. The work clearly attacks the impulses to escape into a magical world of art and to ignore the quotidian demands of life.

Besides being an achieved aesthetic order, the central section of the poem presents an achieved social order. As befits a royal ceremony, each of the characters is shown in his proper relation to others. Having been thrown into one species of

27. Kermode, ed., *The Tempest* (New York: Random House, 1964), 6th ed., p. lxii.

disorder—usurpation—by Prospero's abdication of his civil responsibilities and Antonio's usurpation, the characters are brought to the island. There comic disorder reigns at first, and then, as a result of the proper use of the imagination by Prospero, order is restored; this is the traditional arc of comic art. Since the emergent order results from the proper use of the imagination we are led to consider the role of Ariel. Auden's identification of Ariel with the imagination and his characterization of the imagination as "incapable of distinguishing between permitted and forbidden possibilities" (*DH*, p. 133) make it impossible to see Ariel, as Greenberg does, as representing the cognitive ego; the cognitive ego is represented by the audience, which is, ultimately, the reader. Ariel corresponds, simply, to the imagination, that capacity of the ego that can produce possibilities by its infinite capacity for play. It can, for instance, imagine a well-ordered dukedom ruled by Trinculo with Stephano as heir. Indeed, its capacity for enumerating such possibilities is what makes it useful, its inability to distinguish among them what makes it dangerous and requires that it be governed by the ego when questions of choice arise.

And yet, with all the emphasis on the limitations of art and the imagination, the whole poem is thoroughly governed by the spirit of Ariel: it is a playful work. In a stage production of *The Tempest*, Auden says,

Caliban should be as monstrously conspicuous as possible, and, indeed, suggest, as far as decency permits, the phallic. Ariel, on the other hand, except when he assumes a specific disguise at Prospero's order, e.g., when he appears as a harpy, should, ideally, be invisible, a disembodied voice.   [*DH*, p. 132]

This seems to me exactly what Auden has accomplished. Ariel is constantly present but invisible, Caliban monstrously con-

spicuous. The work is equally a discourse on the limitations
and dangers of art misused and a celebration of its right use:
to make us see; to show us our place; to provide us with possible orders from which to choose as we attempt to transform
immediacy into actuality.

Order is the crucial word: the work continually asks us to
ask what *kind* of order its author has created. In a note to
New Year Letter, Auden defines the artist as "one whose
desire for perfection is *exactly* balanced by his cowardice, his
fear of what the attempt to achieve perfection will involve"
(p. 90). In *The Sea and the Mirror* this balance is continually
evident. The work persistently redefines its own order, enlarges and complicates its own balancing mechanism; it continually advertises its own contrivances, "the mirrors and
wires" by which it works. Thus it "opens the fishiest eye"—
corrects deficient seeing by looking in the most fraudulent
("fishiest") manner—on both itself and ourselves. The reader
is continually made aware of his own position vis-à-vis the
work. The danger of describing the poem's form for itself or
reading its allegory as a message is that no form or statement in
the work stands unqualified by any other. Its form becomes
one of the referents of its allegory, its staging and mirroring
are figures for our own awareness of ourselves. It is impossible,
the work suggests, to understand its substance without following its own complex point of view. Still, there *is* an object to
be understood, a view to be seen, and a model of human existence presented. Caliban's final turns of phrase, describing
man as his own audience, watching his "behaving flesh" that is
"really sore and sorry" and "swaying out on the ultimate
wind-whipped cornice that overhangs the unabiding void"
(*CLP*, p. 249; *SP*, p. 112), are at once fine pieces of verbal
theater and a map of man and his position, the one inseparable
from the other. Caliban, the speaking, acting mountebank of

a monster, who is also his own audience, is present as the image of us all.

In his mature work, Auden emphasizes not the aesthetic strengths but the moral and even perceptual weaknesses of an "objective" perspective. "Memorial for the City" (*CSP*, p. 289), which considers a bleak postwar landscape in relation to the history of man's attempts to build cities—to civilize himself—opens as follows:

> The eyes of the crow and the eye of the camera open
> Onto Homer's world, not ours.   [*CSP*, p. 289]

The differences between this and the perspective of "Consider" are as striking as the similarities, for if the crow and the camera resemble the hawk and the airman in their objectivity, their detachment, their fusion of past with present and of natural with mechanical, they lack—despite or even because of their association with the Homeric—the grandeur of hawk and airman. The poem argues that, as seen by crow and camera, the modern world is Homeric in the sense that

> First and last
> They magnify earth, the abiding
> Mother of gods and men; if they notice either
> It is only in passing.   [*CSP*, p. 289]

The crow and the camera, for all their reputed accuracy of vision, magnify earth and diminish men, almost fail to notice them. They "see as honestly as they know how, but they lie" because they cannot see human suffering and weakness, and cannot acknowledge the potential benefits of suffering and weakness:

> As we bury our dead
> We know without knowing there is reason for what we bear,

That our hurt is not a desertion, that we are to pity
Neither ourselves nor our city.   [*CSP*, p. 290]

The weakness of the crow-camera perspective is that from it one cannot see with full clarity: Auden is endorsing a higher objectivity. In an essay of about the same vintage Auden discusses the shortcomings of an "objective" perspective in detail:

From the height of 10,000 feet, the earth appears to the human eye as it appears to the eye of the camera; that is to say, all history is reduced to nature. This has the salutary effect of making historical evils, like national divisions and political hatreds, seem absurd. . . . Unfortunately, I cannot have this revelation without simultaneously having the illusion that there are no historical values either.   [*DH*, p. 101]

At the same time, man is his own self-corrector; his weakness —the speaker of the fourth part of "Memorial for the City" —will always speak out to declare man's independence from those perspectives that try to show him as an automaton, as the obedient servant of natural law.

The comic perspective is more fully realized in another perspective poem, "In Praise of Limestone" (*CSP*, p. 238; *SP*, p. 114), which discusses, among other matters, the "worldly duty" of a fantasy Eden imagined as a limestone landscape. Here again, the poem gives explicit directions for viewing:

> Mark these rounded slopes
> With their surface fragrance of thyme and, beneath,
> A secret system of caves and conduits; hear the springs
> That spurt out everywhere with a chuckle,
> Each filling a private pool for its fish and carving
> Its own little ravine whose cliffs entertain
> The butterfly and the lizard; examine this region

Of short distances and definite places.

[*CSP*, pp. 238–239; *SP*, p. 114]

The scene is both arbitrary—it could be any set of images—and necessary—for each person it can be only one set of images.

Most simply, this is the world of childish fantasy carried into adulthood. There is a gentle irony throughout, beautifully realized in the speaker's voice: limestone is to be praised precisely because it is malleable; it is both definite ("these solid statues") and indefinite ("it dissolves in water"); the definite indefiniteness of our inner fantasy world makes us unique persons.

What we are asked to view and to praise is a fanciful web of not necessarily related images and actions, praiseworthy precisely because innocent, silly, and, in an important sense, unreal. Objects in this world change immediately as the subject wishes; everything is surface and illusion, and, for just this reason, has the pure reality of a child's daydreams; the mirror of art becomes, here, a door to the other side of the looking glass. Thus neither the poet nor the scientist feels at home:

> The poet,
> Admired for his earnest habit of calling
> The sun the sun, his mind Puzzle, is made uneasy
> By these marble statues which so obviously doubt
> His antimythological myth.   [*CSP*, p. 240; *SP*, p. 116]

That is, the poet works under the myth that he can bring word and image together, that the sun (thing) is "the sun" (word); this is an antimythological belief in that it supposes a wedding of fact and fiction that we do not ordinarily ask of myth; it is still myth because it is, for the poet, more a matter of faith than fact. Similarly, the scientist, as he tries not so much to discover as to codify "Nature's / Remotest aspects," is chased by gamins "with such lively offers"—an image that contrasts the heavy seriousness of science with the innocent lewdness of childhood.

The importance of this Arcadian daydream world rests in its apparent frivolity, triviality, unpredictability, and outlandishness. The point, which Auden argues in many places in many ways, is that the uniqueness of each person, and his capacity for loving, are based, at least in part, on his internal landscape. This landscape, far from reflecting, as it does in so much modern literature, depths of impassioned feeling, is nothing very spectacular: "Among the half dozen or so things for which a man of honor should be prepared, if necessary, to die, the right to play, the right to frivolity, is not the least" (DH, p. 89).

Frivolity, because it is unpredictable and irresponsible, reminds man that there exists no facsimile of himself, and that what the world may well regard as his weaknesses are the bases of his uniqueness. "A sense of humor develops in a society to the degree that its members are simultaneously conscious of being each a unique person and of being all in common subjection to unalterable laws" (DH, p. 372). At the end of "In Praise of Limestone," frivolity has modulated into a quixotic, religious playfulness:

> . . . if
> Sins can be forgiven, if bodies rise from the dead,
>   These modifications of matter into
> Innocent athletes and gesticulating fountains,
>   Made solely for pleasure, make a further point:
> The blessed will not care what angle they are regarded from,
>   Having nothing to hide.   [CSP, p. 241; SP, p. 117]

Characteristically, Auden makes his point in terms of perspective: the blessed will not care what angle they are regarded from. Blessedness, forgiveness, love, resurrection: these are not matters of looking at things in a certain way; each is *sui generis*, and the closest we can come to imagining what they are like is to send our imaginations back to the world of psychomythic Eden. Blessedness, pure innocence, by definition needs no proper perspective, but, since we do not live in a world of essences, we must still look at things from some place.

Perhaps the best way to describe the total perspective of "In Praise of Limestone" is to say that it probes, and accepts, the disproportions and surprises in the relations between the busy world and the fantasy world, the relations among the various functions of the fantasy world, and the relationship between its apparent unimportance and its actual service. Such probing uncovers both political and religious ramifications:

> It has a worldly duty which in spite of itself
>   It does not neglect, but calls into question
> All the Great Powers assume.   [*CSP*, p. 240; *SP*, p. 116]

And it tells something about the importance of distinguishing between what is serious and what is not:

A frivolity which is innocent, because unaware that anything serious exists, can be charming, and a frivolity which, precisely because it is aware of what is serious, refuses to take seriously that which is not serious, can be profound.

Christianity draws a distinction between what is frivolous and what is serious, but allows the former its place. What it condemns is not frivolity but idolatry, that is to say, taking the frivolous seriously.   [*DH*, pp. 429, 430]

"In Praise of Limestone" has a shifting perspective, one that surveys the landscape, sorting out what is serious from what is not. It shows the landscape as a pure fantasy world, then as a slightly salacious land of wish projection, then as the abode of the ordinary, then as a backward, seedy province, then as the bulwark of individuality against the encroachment of the Great Powers, and finally as our best image of ideal love and the forgiveness of sins. Limestone is the correct image because it can represent all of these things; its virtue is that the imagination can shape it as it pleases. Thus we see another characteristic strategy of the comic artist: he lets the imagination run wild. Rather than seeking an accommodation between reality and the imagination, he grants the imagination hegemony within its proper realm (as Prospero frees Ariel) in order to keep the distinction between illusion and reality clear, in order to ridicule the pomposities of overseriousness, and in order to let it give us images of what we might be.[28]

The art by which such acts of the comic imagination lead to clarification and thence to action—love—reaches one of its high points in "Secrets" (*CSP*, p. 318), where perspective is put forward as peeking, humanness as shortsightedness, and true seeing as a matter of perceiving how little we can see:

> That we are always glad
> When the Ugly Princess, parting the bushes
> To find out why the woodcutter's children are happy,
> Disturbs a hornets' nest, that we feel no pity
> When the informer is trapped by the gang in a steam-room,
> That we howl with joy
> When the short-sighted Professor of Icelandic

28. For a careful discussion of the diction of this poem, see Replogle, *Auden's Poetry*, pp. 237–241.

Pronounces the Greek inscription
A Runic riddle which he then translates:

Denouncing by proxy our commonest fault as our worst;
That, waiting in his room for a friend,
We start so soon to turn over his letters,
That with such assurance we repeat as our own
Another's story, that, dear me, how often
We kiss in order to tell,
Defines precisely what we mean by love:—
To share a secret.   [*CSP,* pp. 318–319]

As John Bayley has pointed out, the success of the poem comes in part from its control, "with its long linked succession of subordinate clauses kept perfectly in control until the main verb descends with precision in the sixteenth line." [29] When the predicate to the opening clauses comes, revealing the common denominator to be the sharing of a secret, the reader has been placed in a position that can be defined quite precisely: he is sharing a secret. The unknown has been revealed to him, and the response is exactly that sense of treasured release that comes when we do share a secret; that which has been unknown is made known.

Each of the vignettes presents the human urge to share with others. The poem moves from fantastic, almost slapstick, instances in the first stanza, to personal faults in the second. Before we know it, we are indeed "denouncing by proxy our commonest fault as our worst," and discovering that these faults define what we mean by love.

By the time the speaker announces that "the joke, which we seldom see, is on us," he has already played the joke on us several times. He engages us in peeking at the peekers, shows

29. *Romantic Survival,* p. 174.

us that we do much the same thing, shares the secret that he too has laughed at common human flaws and looked at people's letters, plagiarized jokes, and kissed to tell. He establishes a conspiratorial and then a confessional "we" that finally becomes the "we" of the humble believer:

> The joke, which we seldom see, is on us;
> For only true hearts know how little it matters
> What the secret is they keep:
> An old, a new, a blue, a borrowed something,
> Anything will do for children
> Made in God's image and therefore
> Not like the others, not like our dear dumb friends
> Who, poor things, have nothing to hide,
> Not, thank God, like our Father either
> From whom no secrets are hid.   [CSP, p. 319]

The syntactical legerdemain is still at work, but now it serves neither to enchant nor to reveal, but to define man's place in the order of things, to "thank God" that, whatever odd forms it takes, our humanity carries with it the capacity to love. Even the Ugly Princess, the informer, and the shortsighted professor become worthy of love. By this process of reversal, clarification, and release, and by the progressive education of the reader, stock characters gain an innerness comparable to our own. By sharing with us a number of trivial, but important, secrets, the poem engages us in forgiveness.

Each of the poems discussed in this chapter is a variation on a basic pattern. "A Change of Air," which Auden discusses in answer to a *Kenyon Review* symposium on it,[30] is a paradigmatic example: we go somewhere else to reestablish proper relations between our name and ourselves, and come back the better for it. Each poem is a kind of Italian Journey,

30. 26 (1964), 204–208.

a health cure, not away from things as they really are, but to a point from which we can more clearly see things as they are. It is the traditional pattern of the comic quest, and the quester, if the poems work as they mean to, is ultimately the reader. He journeys into the poem and out again, into the world in which his actions really matter. It is too flexible and too variable a pattern to reduce to a formula, and for all that Auden, as his remarks in the symposium underscore, is one of the most self-conscious of poets, this must be one of those patterns that strongly affect, but lie beneath, conscious intention. It is usually a journey into a world of playful disorder, and our laughter is both our reaction to seeing things as they are and a safety valve against our entering more deeply into the work than we ought, against our desire to remain in a magic world of art. Each poem is Saturnalian, an enlightening, festive, weekend occasion; it is also, in its craft, a week's work. In Freudian terms, the laughter is a release of the energy we have been using to suppress what we think we do not want to know about the way things really are with ourselves and with the world. In Bergsonian terms, it is itself a loosening of our responses so that we may react to the world and continue to evolve. At the moment of comic release, we are out of time: "while we laugh, time stops and no other kind of action can be contemplated" (*DH*, p. 206). Since the duty of the work is not only to clarify relations but to return us to the world of "real" time, in which actions must be chosen, the terminal act of the work of art is to remind us that, although the order and the spirit of charity that it has shown are applicable and desirable in "real time," they can exist there only by our choice and action. The work of art cannot guarantee its own success; it cannot ensure that we will choose well. It can, however, suggest that some kinds of choices and actions are better than others. At the same time, poetry is the result of an activity, the poet's carpentry with words, sentences, figures, and forms; by being well made, the poem provides a reference to the world of nonartistic making, an analogy in which the agent has labored well and with love.

Much of the process of clarification involves gaining objectivity in the root sense of establishing a definable and measurable external world whose existence as something separate from our perceptions of it can be verified. Since many of our actions result not from our own volition but from our subjection to natural laws, both social and biological, one act of clarification is to distinguish where these laws operate and where they do not, the sphere of "behaviour" and the sphere of "deeds." "Freedom is the recognition of necessity": Auden repeatedly quotes Engels on this matter, and one of the functions of the comic imagination is to delineate the world of necessity, to give us the freedom of sobriety, the freedom Prospero symbolically gains when, having lived on an enchanted island, he breaks his wand and gives up trying to humanize Caliban, who represents raw actuality and hence total subservience to natural law. Prospero recognizes an area of freedom and an area of necessity and ceases trying to use his art to correlate them.

This process is a matter not only of vision but also of ethics; there is a prescription not only to see clearly but also to make ethical choices, choices within the arena of an untransfigured reality, within the "ethical dark" in which we live. Choices made outside this arena, choices made on the bases of perceptions of an aesthetically transformed reality, are apt to be wrong choices.

Although the gymnastics of Auden's style often hold our attention, although they are essential to the poems' attempts to "enter history as agents," the substance of the poems is also of great importance. They contain rich and intelligent thematic material, material of which the ostentations of manner are the appropriate means of expression. The point seems obvious enough; I make it because Auden's best recent defenders have thought it useful or necessary to deny it. John Bayley and John Blair, working from different directions, both come to the conclusion that the ideational content of the poems is secondary, perhaps tertiary, perhaps irrelevant, to the general "theatrical" effects of the style. Bayley suggests that Auden's style is richly Romantic, often despite the poet's ostensible attempts to make it otherwise, and that the style has a life quite independent of the persuasive goals of the poems; at best, the stated rhetorical goal is a platform on which to display a romanticist sensibility. Blair suggests that Auden's stylistic flair is a kind of higher didacticism, aiming to impart no specific, discursive truths but rather, by game and indirection, to inculcate a general Kierkegaardian sense of the absence of general truths. Bayley tells us much about Auden's sensibility and Blair much about the rationale behind Auden's characteristic poetic tactics, but both discount the orthodox didactic and persuasive element in his work. The poems discussed here enact discovery, they suggest its richness, and—for all their stylistic elaboration—they recommend it with the full force of simple, clear imperatives and declaratives: Look, stranger, now; The eyes of the crow and the eye of the camera lie; Consider this. There is a steady impulse in the poems toward clarification of both scene *and* statement, and an insistence on both seeing and entering into history. The major goal of much Auden criticism seems to be that of moving the poetry away from history, away from direct statement about and involvement in human events; the poetry itself moves in precisely the opposite direction.

For Auden, poetry is an instrument of discovery, in the root sense in which "discover" is used in the second line of "On This Island": literally, to take the covers off. His poems attempt to be, and I think are, models of elucidation; they both extol and exemplify the search for clarity. In the poems discussed here, the viewer often cannot see clearly without removing himself to a point from which he is in danger of not seeing accurately; he cannot, at the same time, feel fully without risking a distorting involvement. Finally, however, the discipline of viewing well is subordinate to the presentation of man viewing as a fundamental image of man's relation to experience, to his position in the world.

3. Arrangement

In England in the 1930's poetry and politics were unusually responsive to each other; a rhythm or a rhyme or an odd usage could send ripples, and could also be a response to ripples sent by others.[1] In spite of all that has been written about that period, these ripples have not yet been carefully traced, and we tend vastly to oversimplify the ideas embodied in Auden's early poems. For example, *The Orators* was evidently very significant during the thirties; everyone seems to have known what it was about. But, as G. S. Fraser has remarked, one is apt to find, coming back to it years later and in a different context, a meaning quite different from what everyone assumed it to have when it was published.[2]

One can find, nonetheless, in the poetry of this period, the roots of Auden's mature art. The close connection between the arrangements of words in his poems and his philosophical concern with the nature and position of man appears early. Form in the early poems functions in part as a frame on which

1. For an interesting account of this period and these ripples, see Peter Stansky and William Abrahams, *Journey to the Frontier: Two Roads to the Spanish Civil War* (New York: Norton, 1970).

2. "The Career of W. H. Auden," in Spears, *Auden Essays*, pp. 82–86. See also Julian Symons, *The Thirties* (London: Cresset, 1960), p. 14. The political ambiguity of *The Orators* seems in part to reflect political ambiguities existing in England early in the 1930's.

self-qualifying opposites are placed and allowed to interact;
nearly always, the ultimate position arrived at is a familiar
area of complexity and uncertainty, variously described as
"middle-earth," "this island," "the time being," "the ordinary
way."

The short, slant-rhyming lines of "This Lunar Beauty,"
for example, bring together time and timelessness in a series
of concords:

> This lunar beauty
> Has no history,
> Is complete and early;
> If beauty later
> Bear any feature,
> It had a lover
> And is another.   [*CSP*, p. 44; *SP*, p. 8]

Looking at something makes it a part of the observer's world;
to add anything to something already complete is to make it
less complete. If that complete thing "bear any feature" (a
phrase that telescopes "bear any resemblance" and "have any
features whatsoever") it is no longer what it was. Thus, the
existence of the pure and complete can be known only by the
absence of anything by which we, existing in time, could
know it.

The poem compresses these paradoxes into a pattern of abstract words in simple syntactical patterns; its purity of diction, its tone of logical demonstration, its simple phrasing,
seem almost a counterargument to the paradoxes they present;
they create a surface almost as pure as lunar beauty. "Early,"
for instance, is a carefully chosen word. As the feminine off-
rhymes with "beauty" and "history" suggest, it is necessarily
imprecise: no word can perfectly express timelessness, and

the proximate word, deftly used, reveals not the nature of the timeless but our relation to it; "early" is as close as we can get.

The whole poem, in fact, is a tightly woven fabric of time words (history, later, other time, changes, never, finished, endless, and, in one of its senses, lunar) and of various tenses of simple monosyllabic verbs, especially words describing states of being. These accumulate into a Dianan image, whose chastity, beauty, and danger cohere in a contrast to the temporal world, where "time is inches / And the heart's changes," where, using another paradox, time is not temporal.

The poem is a warning, however, not against pure beauty, but, implicitly, against mistaking the temporal world for the atemporal:

> And till it pass
> Love shall not near
> The sweetness here,
> Nor sorrow take
> His endless look.   [*CSP*, p. 44; *SP*, p. 9]

The general sense is clear enough: a fixation on the timeless distracts us from the world of time in which love operates and which, in another fine turn, has its own kind of eternity, sorrow being "endless." The ghost, the ambiguity of the referent of "it," the dream time referred to in the second stanza all help to give the poem a tantalizing quality that, it suggests, inheres in the concept of timelessness. Generally, ambiguity is used with just this precision; by describing the timeless in terms that can only be approximate, a texture of temporality is established; and looking at that which defies observation is valuable because it returns us to that which does not.[3]

Thus the poem makes two points. By its deceptively simple

3. But see John Fuller, *Reader's Guide*, p. 45: the poem "seems to be 'about' a photograph of the loved-one as a child."

language, it suggests that the relation of temporality to atem-
porality is endlessly paradoxical, that, as Auden puts it in
New Year Letter, "we in fact live in eternity," an endless
present in which we can imagine but not know existence out
of time. At the same time, we live in a moral world of prosaic
time and fickle affections, in which, if we are to perform the
offices of love, we must eschew the quest for the timeless and
absolute. Wherever it may stand theologically, the poem is
not very far intellectually from *For the Time Being.*

Every poem Auden writes is an exploration of the possibilities of the linguistic and formal conventions it adopts;
this is one of the reasons it is difficult to characterize his style.
"The Wanderer" (*CSP,* p. 51; *SP,* p. 10), to take another
very early poem, brings together echoes of Anglo-Saxon
poetry and—as suggested by its original title, "Chorus from a
Play," and its division into parts resembling a strophe, antis-
trophe, and epode—of the Greek choric ode. I read the poem
as suggesting that Greek and Anglo-Saxon views of volition
are perhaps more accurate than those we generally hold when
we view questing as an act of individual freedom. The arrangement of series of short phrases in syntactically subordinate juxtapositions, defined by lines and alliteration, is a basic
resource of Auden's art; it is a vehicle of contrast, complement, supplement, and sheer verbal excitement that does not
break the basic linear movement of assertive statement. Auden
seems to have learned much from the Anglo-Saxon about the
organization of phrases.

The opening line is a found object,[4] translated. Its move-

---

4. "Ha beoð se wise þat ha witen alle godes reades. his runes ant
his domes þe derne beoð ant deopre þen ani sea dingle," quoted by
Fuller, *Reader's Guide,* p. 48. Also see Morton W. Bloomfield, "Doom
is dark and deeper than any sea-dingle: W. H. Auden and *Sawles
Warde,*" *Modern Language Notes,* 63 (1948), 548–552.

ment through the four alliterated words, from "doom," with
its present apocalyptic connotations, to "sea-dingle" is striking; our reaction is, what a funny thing for doom to be deeper
than. Auden uses the emphases supplied by the Anglo-Saxon
line to play the threatening and mysterious "dark" and
"deeper" against the almost trivial "sea-dingle." Throughout
the poem Auden is doing exactly what he says he is doing in
his poetry of the fifties and sixties, hymning the English language and playing incessant word games with the reader. He
traces the wanderer's journey through a series of verbal surprises and riddles. I think we have the matter reversed if we
think of Auden as using the ellipses and kennings primarily
to suggest the Anglo-Saxon "style." More important than the
poetic echoes of lines like "A stranger to strangers over un-
dried sea, / Houses for fishes, suffocating water," is the way
words and phrases now in our vocabulary work to create a
texture. "Houses for fishes," a witty kenning (flavored by the
falling rhythm and the faint rhyme, and the use of a plural
vehicle for a singular tenor), makes sense because "houses" is
such an inappropriate term for what the sea is; it is a land term,
and the point is that man is not "at home" on the sea, the
prototypical image of possibility. Similarly, we do not usually
think of "suffocating" as being what water does to nonfishes,
but the use is precise. More importantly, using another land
term to describe water again emphasizes the dangers as well
as the improvidence of wandering. Such word play, which
permeates the poem and is made possible by the Anglo-Saxon
phrasing, points toward the final prayer of the epode: "Bring
joy, bring day of his returning, / Lucky with day approaching, with leaning dawn." The word play, which continually
points to the harshness of nature and to the conflict between
communal values and those of the quest, prepares for the final
invocation for safe return.

Auden seems to have recognized at the very beginning of his career a connection between intricate, playful, rhetorical patterns and simple, direct ethical precepts. He lets verbal misrule reign momentarily as a means of gaining moral clarification. An example in a very different mode is the apparently simple nocturne from the end of Act II of *Dog Beneath the Skin* (the whole play is a journey through disguise and verbal play toward moral clarification). The poem opens with a quirkish but accurate description of perspective:

> Now through night's caressing grip
> Earth and all her oceans slip,
> Capes of China slide away
> From her fingers into day,
> And the Americas incline
> Coasts toward her shadow line.   [*CP*, p. 218]

The personification of night as mistress is also geographically precise. Strictly speaking, it *is* night that "stands still" while earth moves, and the lines' effect comes partly from our recognition that a very conventional, pre-Copernican figure of speech would be acceptable to a modern astronomer.

The poem then shifts from a cosmic to a psychological point of view; through dreams,

> Just and unjust, worst and best,
> Change their places as they rest;
> Awkward lovers lie in fields
> Where disdainful beauty yields;
> While the splendid and the proud
> Naked stand before the crowd,
> And the losing gambler gains,
> And the beggar entertains.   [*CP*, p. 218]

The reversals of the opening lines are amplified and elaborated. The chiasmus of the first couplet quoted summarizes the whole movement: just and unjust do indeed "change their places," just before that phrase occurs, and that they do so "as they rest" completes the movement. Since reversal is the immediate subject—reversal in dreams of all "waking" positions, of beggar, gambler, beauty, and awkward lover—the rhetorical figure is apt and successful. And because the verse moves smoothly and easily, we are apt to ignore how perceptively it yokes the mechanics of dream reversal and those of comic verbal reversal.

The series of orderly reversals prepares us for the final supplication:

> May sleep's healing power extend
> Through these hours to each friend;
> Unpursued by hostile force
> Traction engine bull or horse
> Or revolting succubus;
> Calmly till the morning break
> Let them lie, then gently wake.   [CP, p. 218]

Here the salient item is the triplet: the added line ("Or revolting succubus") stands out like a nightmarish irregularity which is exactly what it describes: the dangerous extreme that the healing cycle of dreams touches. The interruption is not total: the off-rhyme keeps it almost as much within the pattern as without. The two substantive words of the line obtrude, but, in the end, pull the poem together: revolting, of course, is slang for "extremely repellent," but in its root sense continues the image of the earth's revolution from the opening lines. Similarly, succubus, an even more obtrusive image ("a demon supposed to have carnal intercourse with men in their sleep," OED), renews the opening personification of night as a woman. Taken together, the two words say much: by echoing the opening images of the poem, they help to create a circular motion, a revolution, that is capped by the final couplet; they also suggest that, in the natural human cycle, in which—at night, through dreams—the unnatural is a part of the natural balance, reversal is a mechanism of restoration. The contrast of the two forms of revolting and of the succubus with "Night's caressing grip" (complicated by the incongruity of "caressing" and "grip," the loving and the sinister) suggests the dangers of the journey into a world of reversal, just as the deviation from the couplet is a dangerous but necessary excursion from the poetic norm.

With the final couplet, the nocturnal convention of a prayer for peaceful sleep and gentle waking returns, but the ivory and horn gates the poem has taken us through give a fresh sense to the convention: the tone is harmonious, but the harmony is composed of discords and irregularities. The restorative powers of sleep are figured as night the mistress, and the dangers as succubus; Auden suggests that one must venture close to the latter to receive the aid of the former. The dream world is a reversal of the daylit world, and the revolving movement of man through the two is shown to be as natural as the movement of earth; a continuity, or, at least, a similarity, between man and nature is established. In poem after poem, Auden finds conventional material to apply to a fresh situation in such a way as both to throw light on the situation and to reinvigorate the convention, a process which becomes a part of the larger comic task of connecting the aberrant and the normative.

A brief example of the way in which this kind of interplay works to make a statement both texturally and directly is the dedicatory poem to *Look, Stranger!*:

> Since the external disorder, and extravagant lies,
> The baroque frontiers, the surrealist police;

What can truth treasure, or heart bless,
But a narrow strictness? [5]

A great deal happens in this little poem. The threats, as embodied in the four nouns of the first clause, move toward concreteness and menace, from "disorder" to "police." The adjectives governing each noun move toward the irrational (external, extravagant, baroque, surrealist). The discord within each noun-adjective pair grows (external disorder creates little tension, surrealist police, a great deal). And the ratio of stressed to unstressed syllables increases, creating a progressive metrical concentration. The "resolution," in the last two lines, emerges easily from the patterns that describe the menace. The resolution of discord in the direct compound subject and verb ("truth treasure" and "heart bless") suggests both ease of action and a union of heart and truth in a narrow strictness that is not at all claustrophobic. Whatever political or artistic credo or union of the two is suggested by that last phrase, the way in which Auden uses his language and his form to create a complex endorsement of simple moral directness is striking. In each of these early poems interplay between convention and reality, between simplicity of form or sentiment and complexity of elaboration, is thematic as well as formal and stylistic. Elaboration rarely destroys clarity and strictness of statement; it is their vehicle. As Stuart Hampshire has put it, Auden's "lyrical gift was never used to justify a claim to a superior imaginative truth which cannot bear the test of prosaic doubt and of mere common-sense." [6] This view is very much the opposite of Bayley's. Discussing the sonnet "Meiosis" (*CSP*, p. 77) he says that, "with the second line of

5. *Look, Stranger!* (London: Faber & Faber, 1936), p. 7.
6. "Doctor Auden," rev. of *CSP*, *New York Review of Books*, 15 Feb. 1968, p. 3.

the sestet . . . the sonnet becomes all but impenetrable to rational analysis." Nevertheless,

the obscurity does not check and irritate or demand to be sorted out; and we float over it on to the final line with a satisfying impression of the sonnet as a whole. It may not be a very clear impression, but that is part of the poem's technique: indeed it is difficult not to conclude that Auden's purpose in the sestet is to give us the *feeling* of a complex idea rather than presenting such an idea for our rational elucidation; to give us sort of a metaphysical thrill.[7]

Bayley goes on to suggest that Auden is using "an apparently metaphysical exactness of language for its suggestiveness, not for its literal meaning"; and since the function and importance of ideas in Auden's poetry in relation to complex aesthetic structures is a matter of signal importance, it is worth testing Bayley's assertions about the poem's obscurity, and, in fact, looking at the whole poem in detail.

The title alludes to both cytology and rhetoric: meiosis describes the process of cell division that produces daughter cells with half the number of chromosomes present in the original or "mother" cell; it is also a rhetorical term: "To belittle, often through a trope of one word." It can also, as is pertinent here, refer to "litotes," meaning either a "naturally meager style, or one intentionally and aggressively plain."[8] Both the cytological and rhetorical senses are important in the poem; especially important is the correlation of the several senses.

The octave describes the introduction of the sperm into the female and the beginning of its growth through cell division; the sestet considers the implications of the event. The "he"

7. *Romantic Survival*, pp. 165–166; Bayley's italics.
8. Lanham, *Handlist*, p. 65.

of the poem is a male making love, and the "you" is the sperm; this creates a witty dramatic and rhetorical situation. In the first line "he" is trapped by love, a slave to it, fighting for breath (from sexual exertion and also in the sense that life fights for breath to live); in the second line, "he" is struggling, not to free himself, but to possess sexually; "he" forgets his enslavement (line 3) in this "little death" (surrender of freedom and archaic slang for orgasm). "He" is "mother" of the seed (line 4) in that "he" has "given birth" to the sperm; also, in cytology, one speaks of "mother" and "daughter" cells regardless of the sex of the conceived or the conceiving organism. The cell, now addressed as "you," is freed by love (line 5: "through love was free"): the sex act frees the sperm, even though it has never heard of love, being a single cell, and even though the freeing act was one of possession. "You" are free "to take the all-night journey under sea, / Work west and northward, set up building" (lines 7 and 8): this is a metaphor for the sperm's journey in the female as it seeks conception and growth by division. The vehicle of the metaphor is geographical: "While he within his arms a world was holding" (line 6) compares the love partner to a world, establishing the geographical base for a journey metaphor; biologically, this is the beginning of the journey of life.

There is a second sense in which "he" holds "within his arms a world": by sexual embrace "he" is creating another person and, metaphorically, another world. This second sense is expanded in the sestet: "Cities and years constricted to your scope" (line 9). That is, the seed will grow into a person who will exist in time and space; now, the whole future is contained within a microscopic, genetically coded cell. All the sorrows of the living are contained in this cell in simplified form, but they will grow as the child grows and "almost all" of the sorrow "shall be as subtle" when the cell becomes a person. The last lines, however, suggest an area of "hope":

> Yet clearly in that 'almost' all his hope
> That hopeful falsehood cannot stem with love
> The flood on which all move and wish to move.

> [*CSP*, p. 77]

"That 'almost' " refers to the hope that there will be somewhat less sorrow (or sorrow less subtle) for the child than there has been for its parents. (The line is elliptical: "in that 'almost' [is] all his hope.") This hope, paradoxically, is that "hopeful falsehood" will not use love to deceive the child, that the child will accept his place on the "flood" of events, life, and growth, on which he must move and on which, since he too will be a willing captive of love, he will also desire to move.

The poem is about the complexities of love and the paradoxes of freedom and necessity; it is a biological analogue to the Marxian notion of free commitment to deterministic forces. The father of the child (who is the "mother" of the cell) is a slave to love, to natural sexual desires and to love in the sense of life force. This enslavement is, or can be, voluntary, and by it, the "seed" is freed to begin its journey, on and to which it will be a slave: such acceptance defines its freedom. The hope of the parent is that when this seed has, by a process of continual diminution and division (meiotic division), grown into a man, it will accept no false hopes, that this product of a necessary and enslaving love will be free of the deluding notions about freedom and love that might prevent him from freely committing himself to the enslaving flood of evolutionary progress. The child might thus have slightly less subtle sorrows than his parents, and thus be freer in another sense.

This complicated series of paradoxes finds its emblem in the biological model of the dividing cell, which, although minute and helpless, holds within itself the whole future development of the person it will become; which grows by dividing itself into smaller parts; which is freed from the body of its mother at birth but is a slave, in a hereditary sense, to the "mother" cell which produced it and also a slave in that it will be bound to the instinctual forces that led to the sexual act by which it was created.

The rhetorical and stylistic senses of "meiosis" are also important, as they refer both to the poem's restrained manner—the diction is flat and simple, the speaker discusses love in the manner of a zoology lecturer—and to the potential expansion of meaning through this restraint. The sonnet form functions to add another area of reference: it is a tight form, producing its own form of restriction on words; it too gains its expansion of meaning by constriction. It is also conventionally an amatory form, and thus wittily appropriate to the subject, love viewed biologically. Perhaps most remarkably, the sonnet holds two poetic parts in a union that is similar to the way in which, as meiosis occurs, cell division represents the emergence of two discrete parts from a unity. Auden, dealing here with rudimentary poetic matter and rudimentary cellular matter, is suggesting a similarity between the two. The form, then, is one more instance of the interplay of freedom and necessity, and the restatement of this theme in various ways— biological, formal, rhetorical—suggests connections among areas not usually associated. For all that Auden teases the reader by constructing a love sonnet addressed to a spermatozoon, he still maintains scientific precision and, in constructing his figures, uses accurately the facts of cell division; he is not merely creating an illusion of metaphysical exactness, but, on the contrary, is basing the poem on just such exactness.

Poetic discovery and intellectual discovery are rarely at odds in Auden's poetry, a fact that becomes much clearer in the poems written after his return to Christianity and his emigration to America, when the system of beliefs is more sharply defined. The general coordination, however, is present from the beginning. Even in a rather early poem like "Meiosis," which was first published in 1933, we see the basic concerns that have continued to predominate: what is the relation of man as a biological being to man the historical being? How free is man and how does he best exercise his freedom? How does the artist use his art to destroy illusions?

The characteristic mode of the later poems grows naturally from practices present in the earliest poems. "As He Is" (*CSP*, p. 117; *SP*, p. 29; first published, 1940) is a good transitional example. Its subject is Man. He is to be known by being seen in terms of resemblances to and differences from other forms of life. The comparisons take spatial form and man is defined in terms of an environment:

> Wrapped in a yielding air, beside
>   The flower's noiseless hunger,
> Close to the tree's clandestine tide,
>   Close to the bird's high fever,
>   Loud in his hope and anger,
> Erect about a skeleton,
>   Stands the expressive lover,
>   Stands the deliberate man.   [*CSP*, p. 117; *SP*, pp. 29–30]

The poem's wit is the method by which definition and location are arrived at, and the form serves to hold together the multiple coordinates of its definition. "Wrapped" and "yielding" partially contradict each other, but both are true. We approach man by noting all the things that surround him and resemble him, and finally, through what is almost an evolutionary ladder, arrive at the creature, who can stand (meaning "there he is" and that man, unlike other creatures, walks upright), who is "deliberate" (both pauses and thinks), is "expressive" (talks and reveals emotions), and is a "lover" (makes love and can love in a way distinct from all other creatures). Thus the structure of "As He Is" is based on an up-to-date and accurate definition of what is human and where in the ladder of existence humans stand. This use of form persists in Auden's mature poetry and is the source of the poems' arguments and their aesthetic effects. The major developments of the later poetry are simply growth and expansion: the definitions of man's place grow fuller and more precise; the forms grow more intricate and festive; the concord between statement and style grows both larger and more complex.

For the Time Being, first published in 1944 but, according to Spears, written in 1941–1942,[9] marks an attempt to put a view of man into a large, complex form that uses the Christ story as both a parable of humanism and a sanction for the kind of art Auden has always practiced. In a recent essay, Auden talks of the artistic implications of the Incarnation. In a pre-Christian, "magico-polytheistic culture," he says, "poets are the theologians . . . it is they who teach the myths and rescue from oblivion the great deeds of ancestral heroes." The poet

is one whose words are equal to his divine subjects, which can only happen if he is divinely inspired. The coming of Christ in

9. Spears, *Auden*, p. 205.

the form of a servant who cannot be recognized by the eye of
flesh and blood, only by the eye of faith, puts an end to all such
claims. . . . For a poet brought up in a Christian society, it is
perfectly possible to write a poem on a Christian theme, but
when he does so, he is concerned with it as an aspect of a religion,
that is to say, a human cultural fact, like other facts, not as a matter of faith. The poet is not there to convert the world.

The contrast between the claim of the Gospel narratives to be
the Word of God, and the outward appearance and social status
of the characters in them must, if the claim is believed, abolish
the assumptions of the classical aesthetic, as Professor Auerbach
has demonstrated in his remarkable book, *Mimesis*.

[*SW*, pp. 137–138]

Auden goes on to quote Auerbach's analysis of the biblical
account of Peter's denial. Auerbach's point is that the artistic
mixing of styles and usage is both sanctioned and required by
the central events of the Incarnation and the Passion (which
is almost to say that the Bible can be treated as both an artistic
example and an aesthetic tract). Christ comes as a servant, has
as his disciples fishermen and artisans, and is crucified as a
thief. This, Auerbach says,

engenders a new elevated style, which does not scorn everyday
life and which is ready to absorb the sensorily realistic, even the
ugly, the undignified, the physically base. Or—if anyone prefers
to have it the other way around—a new *sermo humilis* is born,
a low style, such as would properly only be applicable to comedy,
but which now reaches out far beyond its original domain, and
encroaches upon the deepest and the highest, the sublime and the
eternal.[10]

10. *Mimesis: The Representation of Reality in Western Literature*,
trans. Willard Trask (Princeton: Princeton University Press, 1953),
p. 72.

The formal organization of *For the Time Being* is directly related to a conception of what Christ's coming to earth as a historical Jesus implies.

The connection is made quite explicitly in "The Meditation of Simeon":

Because in Him the Flesh is united to the Word without magical transformation, Imagination is redeemed from promiscuous fornication with her own images. The tragic conflict of Virtue with Necessity is no longer confined to the Exceptional Hero; for disaster is not the impact of a curse upon a few great families, but issues continually from the hubris of every tainted will. Every invalid is Roland defending the narrow pass against hopeless odds, every stenographer Brünnhilde refusing to renounce her lover's ring which came into existence through the renunciation of love.

Nor is the Ridiculous a species any longer of the Ugly; for since of themselves all men are without merit, all are ironically assisted to their comic bewilderment by the Grace of God. . . .

Nor is there any situation which is essentially more or less interesting than another.   [*CLP*, p. 182]

Simeon goes a step, perhaps a natural step, beyond the strictest theological interpretation of the event. He takes the Incarnation as a grand symbol of the essentially paradoxical relations between finite and infinite, temporal and atemporal, human and divine, word and flesh, and makes it represent the fundamentally paradoxical nature of all existence. Each section of the piece then works out the paradoxicality along some specific coordinate, and the whole work illustrates the central conception of the Incarnation as a "scrambling" event.

The work does not portray the coming of Christ as an announcement of the forgiveness of sins. It is ultimately about the nature of man's existence in the world; it accepts certain aspects of Christian mythology as the best available description of man's nature and situation. In *The Nature and Destiny of Man*, which Auden read at about the time of the composition of *For the Time Being*, Reinhold Niebuhr makes the following general characterization of the importance of the coming of Christ:

Standing in his ultimate freedom and self-transcendence beyond time and nature, [man] cannot regard anything in the flux of nature and history as his final norm. Man is a creature who cannot find a true norm short of the nature of ultimate reality. This is the significance of the historic doctrine of Christ as the "second Adam." The same Christ who is accepted by faith as the revelation of the character of God is also regarded as the revelation of the true character of man. Christ has this twofold significance because love has this double significance.

This "ultimate reality" is neither an "unmoved mover" nor an "undifferentiated eternity" but "the vital and creative source of life and the harmony of life with life," summed up by the phrase "God is love." But, Niebuhr continues, "the essence of human nature is also love, which is to say that for man, who is involved in the unities and harmonies of nature but who also transcends them in his freedom, there can be no principle of harmony short of love in which free personality is united in freedom with other persons." When Auden wrote *For the Time Being* he had at hand a view of the Incarnation as a revelation of man's nature, a clarification of man's obligations to act in the historical context in which he finds himself, and a correction of secular liberal humanism. Liberal humanism is presented here in the character of Herod, and it needs correction not because it is liberal or humane but because, as Niebuhr puts it, "Man is not measured in a dimension sufficiently high or deep to do full justice to either his nature or his capacity for both good and evil or to understand the total environment in which such a stature can understand, express and find itself." [11] *For the Time Being* celebrates the Incarnation as a revelation of man's relation to himself, to time, and to nature, as an answer to a crisis in man's knowledge of himself. Far from resolving paradoxes, it suggests that they are at the heart of man's existence, that Christ, as "second Adam," shows man that existing in time as both a natural creature and a free being is not to be lamented.

The complex sense of time is one of the work's major achievements. Essentially the same sense of time present in early poems like "This Lunar Beauty" and "Musée des Beaux Arts," it has several sources: the use of the medieval tableau, with events presented not as continuous history but as successive instances; the constant shifting of temporal perspective from past to present and back; and the tone of the narrator's final speech. The difference between "As He Is" and *For the Time Being*—if we can compare works of such dissimilar scope—is the degree to which the philosophy of the Incarnation in the latter breeds a thorough mixing of styles. The intent of the two is much the same: to define man as a certain kind of creature existing in a certain kind of world, and the methods are not dissimilar. Among the fullest embodiments of these intentions is the relaxed, informal, meditative ode, generally Horatian in manner. Perhaps more than any other form it has allowed Auden to practice his art fully without committing any of the artistic heresies that his criticism defines.

Two influences seem to be particularly strong. Evidently, as I noted in the discussion of "On This Island," Auden began experimenting with syllabic verse as early as 1935, when

11. *The Nature and Destiny of Man* (London: Nisbet, 1941), I, 157–158, 133.

he first read Marianne Moore. His essay on her (*DH*, pp. 296–305) and his recent poem, "A Mosaic for Marianne Moore" (*CWW*, p. 24), indicate that he has continued to read her poems with admiration. Less traceable, but probably more important, has been the reading of Horace's odes; again, a recent poem, "The Horatians" (*CWW*, p. 26; *SP*, p. 221), affirms and displays the influence.

In both instances, a certain temperamental congeniality, especially for a low-keyed but sharp-eyed approach to the world, and a high degree of respect for poetic making are evident. Almost everyone assumes that true Horatian verse cannot be written in English, or in any uninflected language, or perhaps not in any language except Latin: the great virtue of Latin, on which so many of Horace's effects depend, is the freedom to arrange words for poetic effect without loss of meaning, an effect which cannot as such be produced in a language in which sentence sense depends largely on word order. As Nietzsche puts it:

> Up to this day I have not had an artistic delight in any poet similar to that which from the beginning an Ode of Horace gave me. What is here achieved is in certain languages not even to be hoped for. This mosaic of words, in which every word, by sound, by placing, and by meaning, spreads its influence to the right, to the left, and over the whole; this minimum in extent and number of symbols, this maximum thereby achieved in the effectiveness of the symbols, all this is Roman, and believe me, elegant par excellence.[12]

Auden himself attains such effects not by making English more Latinate, but by recognizing the possibilities of his own language. He writes formal poems in an informal tone of great

12. Quoted and trans., Steele Commager, *The Odes of Horace: A Critical Study* (New Haven: Yale University Press, 1962), p. 50.

subtlety and range of modulation. He creates forms that allow for intricate play of diction and figure without loss of a clear line of "prosaic argument." The poems are alive and moving, and yet have that "feel" of permanence so striking in Horace's odes.

We can see the art of elaborate arrangement in "In Transit," which, by its mosaic of oppositions, develops the occasion of landing at a strange airport into a meditation on man's position:

> Let out where two fears intersect, a point selected
>   Jointly by general staffs and engineers,
> In a wet land, facing rough oceans, never invaded
>   By Caesars or a cartesian doubt, I stand,
> Pale, half asleep, inhaling its new fresh air that smells
>   So strongly of soil and grass, of toil and gender,
> But not for long: a professional friend is at hand
>   Who smiling leads us indoors . . .   [*CSP*, p. 237]

The poem achieves many of the effects of Latinate syntax but retains the relative informality of the middle style. Partly because there is no obtrusive pattern of stressed and unstressed syllables, partly because of the alternation of the flexible eleven and thirteen syllable lines, partly because of the relatively simple vocabulary, there is none of the grandiosity we mistakenly think of as a necessary result of Latinate syntax.

Just as Milton uses complex orderings of words to picture the vast interlocking system of forces active in his epic and the cosmos it portrays, so Auden's deft, subtly complex syntax traces the forces that define his very different view of man's medial position. In the first stanza, the simple subject and verb, "I stand," stands at mid-stanza drawing together and organizing the phrases that indicate the outer limits of that position: "two fears intersect"; the point at which the speaker stands is

"selected / Jointly by general staffs and engineers"; it is between land and ocean, at the meeting point of air culture and
land culture; the speaker is "half asleep." Every coordination,
like "soil and grass" and "toil and gender," and all the words
of intersection and position—jointly, point, facing, at hand—
emphasize and complicate the speaker's in-betweenness.

The pattern of internal rhymes helps to create both the
music and the spatial pattern of the poem. It almost serves as
a system of inflections, drawing words together across the patterns of line and phrasing; it draws our attention to connections and resemblances, which, because the pattern is neither
schematic nor familiar, as in end-rhymed forms, come to the
reader as sudden discoveries. In the first stanza, the rhymes
and half-rhymes (intersect and select, point and jointly,
land, stand, and at hand, Caesar and cartesian, pale and inhale,
new and who, soil and toil) bring phrases and tones together; we are pulled by the latter rhyme word back to the
former and shown a new connection. Linear and spatial form
play against each other; the pattern of linkages is the vehicle
of a definition of man's position.

The next stanzas draw a contrast between "here" and
"somewhere," which looks at first like a simple contrast between the airport and the traveler's destination:

> Somewhere are places where we have really been, dear spaces
>   Of our deeds and faces, scenes we remember
> As unchanging because there we changed, where shops have
>   names,
>   Dogs bark in the dark at a stranger's footfall
> And crops grow ripe . . .   [CSP, p. 237]

The rhyming intensifies, especially with three sounds: places,
spaces, faces, case, and place; heed, needs, and plead; and un-

changing, change, and changed. A major contrast develops
between the antiseptic "now," the moment of the poem, and
the significant "then," represented by words charged with
emotion: change, deed, face, names, crops, kind, protection,
affection, need, plead, place. Auden maps the kind of landscape described in *New Year Letter*—the "landscape of significant action"—with a tinge of wistful nostalgia, as if it were
both more and less "real" than "now." He continues to do so
in the fourth stanza, with the landscape presented as a series
of frontiers, of crucial moments of the intersection of past
and present, unique for each person. The landscape and the
frontier are again contrasted to "this place" in the fifth stanza,
where, in a sense, nothing is real:

> . . . here we are nowhere, unrelated to day or to Mother
>   Earth in love or in hate; our occupation
> Leaves no trace on this place or each other who do not
>   Meet in its mere enclosure but are exposed
> As objects for speculation.   [*CSP*, p. 238]

Here, everyone is a person only as defined by airline manage-
ment, and the physical setting, the hygienic airport, the plate
glass, the lists of names, serve as a landscape of nonbeing,
where people are only parts of a crowd, separated from themselves and from each other. At the same time, this "now," this
moment of being in transit, suggests an extreme instance of
the present here-and-now point we always actually live in.
The frontiers of decision and landscapes of significant events
and actions are more concrete, more compelling, more mem-
orable, but we always live in a moment of incomplete involvement in either a numinous past or a knowable future. Hence,
the airport is a double emblem: it suggests our destructive
separation from what is most real to our minds and also rep-

resents our experience of time as in-betweenness and of space as separation.

The last stanza draws together the various opposites in a contrast of earth and air that restates man's axial position. A disembodied voice

> . . . calls me again to our plane and soon we are floating above
>   A possessed congested surface, a world: down there
> Motives and natural processes are stirred by spring
>   And wrongs and graves grow greenly.   [*CSP*, p. 238]

The mixing of the worlds of history and nature is signalled by the rhymes, which bring the two worlds indiscriminately together, and by our sense of pattern as kaleidoscopic, so that all events—motives or natural processes, wrongs and graves and growing things—appear to be like "the debacle of a river."

The poem grows easily through the meditative tone, speculative movement, and steady transforming of image into emblem. It is not an attack on our "new culture of the air," nor a simple celebration of nature, nor a celebration of then and there as against here and now. The antiseptic airport, the time in transit, are figures, synecdoches, for our condition as conscious beings in time and space: both part of and separate from history, nature, sky, earth, past, future. Every stanza, in rhyme, meter, phrasing, and sense, reiterates and elaborates this middle position. Like so many of the perspective poems, this one leads us through a series of shifts of perspective to tell us not simply what we see from any given point, but where we "really" are.

That quality of voice that we so readily identify as late Auden, although it is actually a tone that is capable of great modulations within and among poems, is clearly a part of the statement. It situates us where the images and devices of perspective locate us; it makes its own statement about the human position. It is also, as Auden makes clear in his recent "The Horatians" (*CWW*, p. 26; *SP*, p. 221), a device of perspective:

> You thought well of your Odes, Flaccus, and believed they
> would live, but knew, and have taught your descendants to
>   say with you: "As makers go,
>   compared with Pindar or any
>
> of the great foudroyant masters who don't ever
> amend, we are, for all our polish, of little
>   stature, and, as human lives,
>   compared with authentic martyrs
>
> like Regulus, of no account. We can only
> do what it seems to us we were made for, look at
>   this world with a happy eye
>   but from a sober perspective."
>
> [CWW, p. 28; SP, p. 223]

The disclaiming and self-qualifying manner is a part of the design of the poems, inseparable from the elements of form and language that are moderating between extremes. Rather than an expression of either false or genuine modesty, the tone is one more device that casts light on man's position. "Foudroyant" is not an absolute poetic virtue; the middle style has its own sublime, and Auden often touches it. The "I" in these poems, with his characteristic refusal to overstate, functions both as an observer and as an example of the human center of consciousness. The speaker in "In Transit" is an instance of in-betweenness; he is in between observation of the external and knowledge of the internal, and the tone, as much as any other element, dramatizes this middle zone, the human point of being that exists between necessity and total freedom. "Little stature" has two senses, one of which suggests a Hobbit-like modesty.

Ultimately, these tonal qualities are part of the attempt to establish a human scale which has been at the heart of Auden's efforts since the earliest poems. In the odes, perspective is again important, not just in the sense of vantage point, but also in the classic sense of just proportion. Poetically, the aerial position is the vantage point from which just proportion can be recognized. Symbolically, it represents a "new culture," not just physical position but a whole set of new assumptions. As such it is a critique of the distorting perspectives, of the "flight from earth" characteristic of post-Renaissance man. This historical sense of perspective appears again in "Ode to Gaea," which opens with a combination of the image of the mirror and the definition of aerial perspective:

> From this new culture of the air we finally see,
> far-shining in excellence, what our Mother, the
>   nicest daughter of Chaos, would
>   admire could she look in a glass,
>
> and what, in her eyes, is natural.   [*CSP*, p. 251]

The coordination is similar to that at the opening of "Memorial for the City": the old and the new are linked as the poem asserts that our modernity, with its presumptions of clear sight and objectivity, now allows us, even forces us, to see things just as the most ancient of viewers—the daughter of Chaos—might see them. The poem is very precise, almost finicky, about perspective. What we see from the air is not simply earth but what personified Earth, could she look in a glass, would "admire" and "what, in her eyes, is natural."

The personification of earth, although it helps to create a style that we might loosely call affected, is not simply an affectation. It is, rather, the first of a series of suggestions that "naturalism" can be a form of distorting and self-deceiving fancy. The image of a daughter admiring herself in a vanity mirror, reinforced by the parenthetical "in her eyes," suggests not wilful distortion but a certain amount of selectivity. The association of ancient myth and modern science implies that scientific objectivity exercises the same kind of benign selectivity of detail that a "young" woman ("the nicest daughter of Chaos") does before her mirror: blemishes and irregularities are explained away or transformed.

This combined view reveals a scene described, appropriately, in terms at once precise and fanciful:

> . . . it is the old
> grand style of gesture we watch as, heavy with cold,
>   the top-waters of all her
>   northern seas take their vernal plunge,
>
> and suddenly her desolations, salt as blood,
> prolix yet terse, are glamorously carpeted
>   with great swatches of plankton,
>   delicious spreads of nourishment,
>
> while, in her realm of solids, lively dots expand,
> companionship becomes an unstaid passion and
>   leaves by the mile hide tons of
>   pied pebbles that will soon be birds.
>
>   [*CSP*, pp. 251–252]

Geographical and anthropomorphic description fuse; a point is made by the intentional mistakes (people and other creatures are "lively dots" and birds' eggs are "pied pebbles") and by the riddles, which create a far from objective style. Words like glamorously, plankton, delicious, and unstaid, instance both the vanity of earth (we are still seeing what she would admire if she could look) and the imprecision of a mock-scientific point of view. Yet the descriptions have their precision. They describe what is "actually seen," for it is an act of intellect and not of observation that enables us to know that the pied pebbles are really birds' eggs; and they give us a sense of the way in which perspective distorts. Coupled, they give a sense of "what is really there."

The imperfection of the adopted point of view is then made explicit:

> Now that we know how she looks, she seems more mysterious
> than when, in her *partibus infidelibus*,
>   we painted sizzling dragons
>   and wizards reading upside down,
>
> but less approachable.   [*CSP*, p. 252]

The phrase "how she looks" continues our double sense of seeing both primary and mirror images: we know "how earth sees," or would see, herself; we know "what she looks like" from a distance. Given the opening stanzas, the suggestion that there was less mystery and more hospitality (the poem does not say more accuracy) in the old maps is not surprising. This stanza also introduces the new image of cartography for perspective. Man watching the earth is a map-maker, and the way in which we make maps tells us more about our abstract image of the earth than about the earth itself. Ancient cartography is no more or less accurate than modern. The question is how and to what extent our ways of looking at the earth humanize or fail to humanize it.

The poem goes on to make the point made in the last stanza of "In Transit." The speaker asks "how does she rank wheel-wrights?" to indicate that earth cannot perceive the products of man the maker, cannot know supranatural, historical things:

> One doubts if she knows
> which sub-species of folly is peculiar to those
>   pretty molehills, where on that
> pocket-handkerchief of a plain

the syntax changes.   [*CSP*, p. 252]

Again, the perspective is trickier than it looks. First, it is actually a perspective on perspectives: we look at ourselves, at earth, and at others looking. Second, the diction keeps shifting from the natural to the historical to the human: when a plain is described, from earth's point of view, as being a pocket-handkerchief, we are not seeing earth from earth's point of view, nor, so far as that goes, from man's, since there is a distortion of scale. Most precisely, we look at ourselves look at earth, and imagine how she would look to herself could she see herself from our position; we betray our own inability fully to adopt a natural point of view. Thus the poem simultaneously makes two points. First, when one sees earth from on high, it doesn't much matter where the syntax changes (hence the comic musings of the "tired old diplomat" who tries to adjust his language and his euphemisms to the quickly changing topography: "Should he / smile for 'our great good ally', scowl / at 'that vast and detestable empire' " [*CSP*, p. 152] and so on). Second, from the sky, the physical residue of history looks like a curious combination of Lyell and Tolkien:

> . . . two lines of moss
>   show where the Devil's Causeway
> drew pilgrims thirteen gods ago,
>
> and on this eve of whispers and tapped telephones
> before the Ninth Catastrophe, square corner-stones
>   still distinguish a fortress
>   of the High Kings from untutored rock.
>
> [*CSP*, pp. 252–253]

When one has viewed history as nature, or both from a point of view from which one cannot distinguish them, the musing leads naturally to a temptation:

> Tempting to mortals is the fancy of half-concerned
> Gods in the sky, of a bored Thunderer who turned
>   from the Troy-centred grief to
>   watch the Hippemolgoi drink their milk,
>
> and how plausible from his look-point . . .   [*CSP*, p. 253]

Having reached the position where real suffering is seen as a natural event, one that is not really related to him and belongs to the same order as that of mythical beasts, the viewer is tempted to retain that separation, to continue not to make the humanly important distinctions. This is the temptation of an objectivist age. Contrasted to this quasi-heroic unconcern is the trivial, yet humane perspective, represented by good manners and easy riddles, that the language of the poem has been insinuating all along. Our lack of skill in answering such riddles indicates the momentary success of the latest threat to the human scale:

> So we were taught

> before the Greater Engines came and the police
> who go with them.   [*CSP*, p. 253]

How to make earth as approachable and unmysterious, as
clearly adapted to the human scale as it was when there was
a preindustrial, pretechnological order to things, when manners were sufficient and reflective of morals; how, in fact, to
save the earth—these are the serious questions asked. The
answer is, in Stephen Spender's phrase, seriously unserious:

> perhaps a last stand in the passes will be made
> by those whose Valhalla would be hearing verse by Praed
>   or arias by Rossini
>   between two entrées by Carême.

> We hope so. But who on Cupid's Coming would care to bet?
> More than one World's Bane has been scotched before this, yet
>   Justice during his *Te Deum*
>   slipped away sighing from the hero's pew,

> and Earth, till the end, will be Herself.   [*CSP*, p. 254]

It is important not to reduce the argument of "Ode to
Gaea" to a simple, logical paraphrase, because its fanciful, elliptical logic, its verbal playfulness and operatic gestures, presented in the well-made Horatian stanzas, are its essence. The
Greater Engines and the police who go with them—modern
industrial-technological society and the semiauthoritarian,
managerial state—are an especially potent threat. The wise,
stern, and large-hearted, traditional defenders of man and
the earth, have not been successful defenders in this instance;
they have been either impotent or seduced, and some even
talk the language of the Engines (something this poem stead-
fastly refuses to do). Perhaps the only available response is
the almost Chaplinesque gesture: a pass defended not by the

self-righteous, so capable of self-delusion, but by the quirkishly eccentric, who not only like but act in terms of good light verse, florid arias, and high cuisine and who are further comforted by the fact that earth will be herself. Only Amphion has "moved her" (his "moving" music moved enough earth to create a fortress), and the orators, those of high period, have always "misled" (fooled and given poor leadership to) democracy. "Our good landscapes"—what we, the lovers of Praed, Rossini, and Carême, the party of useful frivolity—impose on earth are lies but nondestructive and knowing lies. These lies have not altered the surface of the earth, as the machines have, and they are expressions of human uniqueness, which is what the Greater Engines most oppose.

The surface of playful language and runic logic of "Ode to Gaea" is an example of good verbal landscape, the product of humanity viewed as *homo ludens* and *homo faber*, the enemies of the State, which wishes to reduce all humanity and uniqueness to purely natural stuff, as much a fallacy as trying to suppose that Earth is anything but "the real one." We accept the argument only if we follow and accept the purposefully playful form it takes. The poet presses the point, as if to say, if one thinks I'm being frivolous talking about good meals, light verse, and Italian opera at a time like this, he is probably right; but at least I haven't sold out, and, if there is any defense against our modern confusion of history and nature—which is what is presented in the first part of the poem and is the "fallacy of misplaced concreteness" on which the managerial state bases its actions—it is just such spirited frivolity, which has its own special kind of integrity. Thus, the poem ends with not only a defense but a clarification: the earth *is* the earth, our landscapes *are* landscapes, and the two are not to be confused.

Much of the art of "Ode to Gaea" lies in the careful placing of words within stanzas that creates the continual play of meanings and perspectives and, especially, the tone that is so important a part of the poem's argument. Patterning is the method and also a major subject of the poem: it looks at kinds of map-making, and at their relations to the mapped entity, the earth to which it pays homage; the poem is, in fact, almost a history of cartography. Its linear design, like many of the odes, is less easily described. Like "In Praise of Limestone" and "Ischia," it appears to get at its points not by a line of clear argument but by an easy and almost whimsical ambling. In "Ode to Gaea," we get a sense of both historical and geographical panorama, both paralleling the meditative line of the speaker. It moves from perspective to mapping to action, but there is always a double sense created by the original positioning: air is to earth as are our various maps and personifications to the earth; recognizing this is an act of clarification and a defense of what is human.

Just as, to discuss Earth, Auden adopts an aerial perspective, so to discuss History, in "Homage to Clio" (*CSP*, p. 307), he places a speaker in the world of nature, the world of nonhistory. In both instances, we are aware that neither realm can really be separated from the other, that, although distinctions can be made, we are complex creatures living in a double world, constantly in danger of confusing the one with the other.

"Homage to Clio" opens with an observation of seasonal change, of the life of flowers, then of birds making noises, and then of the birds observing the speaker. It constructs an evolutionary ladder that leads to a definition of the world of history.

> More lives than I perceive
> Are aware of mine this May morning

As I sit reading a book, sharper senses
  Keep watch on an inedible patch

Of unsatisfactory smell, unsafe as
  So many areas are: to observation
My book is dead, and by observations they live
  In space, as unaware of silence

As Provocative Aphrodite or her twin,
  Virago Artemis, the Tall Sisters
Whose subjects they are.   [*CSP*, p. 307]

The casual situation of the speaker is made into a figure for the human situation. A man reading a book in a garden, surrounded by the noise and the images of constant reproduction of the realm of nature and at the same time by the silence of history, is man in and out of nature. His voice is the instance of action in the world of time, action that cannot be the same as noise in the realm of nature.

The poem's contrast of the twin goddesses of nature, Artemis and Aphrodite, with the madonna of silences, Clio, is crucial. That there are twin goddesses of nature and a singular goddess of history is definitive, for nature is the realm in which duplication can occur, history the realm of singular occurrence. The comparison is more complicated. In "The Virgin & The Dynamo," Auden writes:

Henry Adams thought that Venus and the Virgin of Chartres were the same persons. Actually, Venus is the Dynamo in disguise, a symbol for an impersonal natural force, and Adam's [*sic*] nostalgic preference for Chartres to Chicago was nothing but aestheticism; he thought the disguise was prettier than the reality, but it was the Dynamo he worshiped, not the Virgin.

[*DH*, p. 63]

The Virgin here is identical with Clio in the poem, and the iconography is important: nature is ruled, in the poem, by twin goddesses, of love and of chastity; history, by the singular madonna, who is both mother and virgin. In the world of nature, love and chastity are identical and iterative, whereas, in the world of history, time is always virginal, since until experienced it is unexperienced. But it also has a productive capacity that differs from that of the chaste natural world, which can only iterate production.

Because the world of nature is a world of repeated events, because it is governed by goddesses rather than a madonna, the world of Aphrodite and Artemis can be easily represented (an act of duplication) in art ("They / Can be represented in granite"); but, the speaker asks,

> . . . what icon
> Have the arts for you, who look like any

> Girl one has not noticed and show no special
> Affinity with a beast?   [*CSP*, p. 309]

Moreover, since she is madonna of silences, to pay homage to her in words is difficult:

> Lives that obey you move like music,
> Becoming now what they only can be once,
> Making of silence decisive sound: it sounds
> Easy, but one must find the time.   [*CSP*, p. 309]

As Robert Bloom points out, there is an intricate figure of speech here: to "find the time" means to achieve rhythm, to recognize the nature of time, and, in the world of constant becoming, to take the time to act decisively.[13]

13. "W. H. Auden's Bestiary of the Human," *Virginia Quarterly Review*, 42 (1966), 225.

The answer to the quandary is personal speech, which means acceptance of the uniqueness of individual beings and the uniqueness of every human act; the reward is that time is the medium of forgiveness. The final prayer—"forgive our noises / And teach us our recollections" (*CSP*, p. 309)— places the poem's focus squarely, as Bloom suggests, on the history of the individual rather than on history in the broad sense. This focus is very much in keeping with the governing assertion of the poem, that in the realm of time it is the uniqueness of the individual person, the individual moment, and the individual act that is important. The same point is made in "Makers of History," which argues, in brief, that the makers of history are not the historical great; they are "those who bred [the Great] better horses, / Found answers to their questions, made their things . . ." (*CSP*, p. 298).

A poem that celebrates the muses of silence and of the unique act and person should be in no way noisy, and should embody a discernible human voice; hence the poem's restrained tone and low-keyed rhetoric. The form and, perhaps, above all, the tone of the meditative ode issue directly from concern with man as a creature existing simultaneously in these realms, with the voice and the situation of the speaker as a major instance of man's in-betweenness.

The systems of oppositions are neither simple nor repetitive. Each poem is a fresh exploration of man's position, a new attempt to try to show man where he is. Thus, "Ode to Terminus" (*CWW*, p. 97) opens by locating man between the macro- and micro-scopic worlds of the scientist:

> The High Priests of telescopes and cyclotrons
> keep making pronouncements about happenings
>   on scales too gigantic or dwarfish
>   to be noticed by our native senses,

discoveries which, couched in the elegant
euphemisms of algebra, look innocent,
    harmless enough but, when translated
    into the vulgar anthropomorphic

tongue, will give no cause for hilarity
to gardeners or housewives: if galaxies
    bolt like panicking mobs, if mesons
    riot like fish in a feeding-frenzy,

it sounds too like Political History
to boost civil morale, too symbolic of
    the crimes and strikes and demonstrations
    we are supposed to gloat on at breakfast.   [*CWW*, p. 97]

The opening perspective is wryly anthropological. The first
stanza poises "high priests" against "native senses," as if science were a form of primitive religion, which, indeed, is part
of the point. Auden, for all his knowledge of science, has always treated it as if it were lore. "Scales" in the third line
balances "gigantic" and "dwarfish," thus establishing a middle
position between microcosm and macrocosm: scales suggests
both balance and proportion. Giant and dwarf are distorted
and abnormal images of man, and yet, by their identification
with the fairy tale, distortions that reveal themselves to be
such. "Native senses" has several meanings. It asserts, as Auden
has always done, the primacy of the phenomenal world. As he
puts it in "Words and the Word," an essay that is an excellent
gloss on this poem:

  We seem to have reached a point where, if the word *real* can
  be used at all, then the only world which is 'real' for us, as the
  world in which all of us, including scientists, are born, work, love,
  hate and die, is the primary phenomenal world as it is, and always

has been, presented to us through our senses, a world in which the sun moves across the sky from east to west, the stars are hung like lamps in the vault of heaven, the measure of magnitude is the human body, and objects are either in motion or at rest.

If this be accepted, it is possible that artists may become both more modest and more self-assured, that they may develop both a sense of humour about their vocation and a respect for that most admirable of Roman deities, the god *Terminus*.   [*SW*, p. 144]

"Native senses," then, are the faculties by which we observe the world in which we live and in which, as in any humanism, the human body is the primary measure of magnitude. "Native" also is a part of a comparison of modern science with primitive magic; and it also suggests common sense, as opposed to the bogey world of giants and dwarves, mesons and galaxies.

In the second and third stanzas of "Ode to Terminus," "native" takes on a new sense, as attention turns to the "elegant / euphemisms of algebra," and the "vulgar anthropomorphic / tongue": native here has to do with various kinds of language. The sense of "vulgar" shifts with the stanza break, from "crude" to "common," "spoken by anyone." "Anthropomorphic," used to describe speech, reinforces our sense of a human scale, and "translation" emerges as a major theme of the poem. The examples of translation in the third stanza create a mock chain of being, from galaxies to mesons, from mob to fish, with housewives and gardeners (creators of order and caretakers of the human scale) in between. Thus, translation is coordinated with the theme of human scale: science, like a fairy tale, is a language that exceeds the ordinary limits of human speech.

The next seven stanzas contrast the make-believe world of the High Priests with the world "we really live in"—"Middle-

/ Earth" (the enjambment makes us see Middle-Earth spatially). Translation occurs as the poem tells the story of the creation of the earth in a quirkish and "vulgar" diction:

> How trite, though, our fears beside the miracle
> that we're here to shiver, that a Thingummy
>   so addicted to lethal violence
>   should have somehow secreted a placid
>
> tump with exactly the right ingredients
> to start and to cocker life, that heavenly
>   freak for whose manage we shall have to
>   give account at the Judgment, our Middle-
>
> Earth . . .   [*CWW*, p. 98]

Middle-Earth is both the real phenomenal world and, by allusion, the benignly fanciful world of Tolkien, itself a world of dwarves and giants. Scientific language is translated into "the vulgar anthropomorphic / tongue." This translation does not dispute the scientific account of creation, but it mocks the dehumanizing language of science.

The poem neither attacks science nor endorses primitive world views, but uses language at once human in scale and rich in variety, capable of being translated. Such language and the sanity it embodies depend in part on our recognition of the nature and dimensions of our home, Middle-Earth, which,

>   . . . whatever micro-
>   biology may think, is the world we
>
> really live in and that saves our sanity,
> who know all too well how the most erudite

mind behaves in the dark without a
    surround it is called on to interpret,

how, discarding rhythm, punctuation, metaphor,
    it sinks into a driveling monologue,
        too literal to see a joke or
        distinguish a penis from a pencil.   [*CWW*, p. 98]

Monologue is speech that no one else hears, the opposite of disclosure. We, we who have lived in the twentieth century, know, even scientifically, what happens to mind alone, acting without a "surround," an environment of definite places and limits. Auden espouses a naive realism on moral and psychological, not epistemological, grounds; when the language of mesons and galaxies becomes reality we have both nuclear warfare and the destruction of the world conceived as man's home. Failure to distinguish penis and pencil is a way of saying that the worlds of nature and of human speech are not to be confused (the illustration is one more translation, one more play on "vulgar"); the failure is both aesthetically and biologically disastrous.

The god of Middle-Earth is Terminus—"God of walls, doors and reticence"—who gives us "games and grammar and meters," the tools of disclosure of self to others:

By whose grace, also, every gathering
    of two or three in confident amity
        repeats the pentecostal marvel,
            as each in each finds his right translator.   [*CWW*, p. 99]

"What happened at Pentecost," Auden explains in "Words and the Word," was "a miracle of instantaneous translation. . . . The curse of Babel, one might say, was redeemed because, for the first time, men were willing in absolute fullness of heart to speak and to listen, not merely to their sort of person but to total strangers" (*SW*, p. 139). Translation images human love; conversely, human love is the means by which God discloses Himself on earth, and depends on language scaled to human need.

The enemy of the world in which Pentecostal translation, representing any act of personal disclosure, may occur is "colossal immodesty." The phrase illustrates the point by its redundancy: immodesty is colossal, that is, beyond the human scale, and it is the immensity of our immodesty that is, literally, ruining the middle earth in which we live. The "self-proclaimed poets," who, "to wow an / audience, utter some resonant lie" (*CWW*, p. 99), are most likely to be guilty of such immodesty; scientists, on the other hand, "remind us to take all they say as a / tall story" (*CWW*, p. 99). We have here the familiar play of limitation with elaboration and of unity with diversity, with the language of the poem, full of numerous acts of translation, as the chief example of its own argument. The walls, doors, and reticence of Terminus are penetrated but left standing.

In Auden's later poems, Pentecost, both the biblical event and the religious festival, is uniquely important. It represents the descent of the Spirit and the possibility of communication among strangers; more precisely, it represents communication as the result of the Spirit's presence in the world. It reaffirms the message of the Incarnation, which, as presented in *For the Time Being*, links the union of finitude and infinity to the mixing of artistic styles.

As Auden presents the event, Pentecost affirms the coherence of truth: the gospel of grace, love, and forgiveness is the same in various tongues, dialects, and styles, and hence the same for all people. It also affirms the tangential but clear relation of different rites and laws to a central body of truth. Pentecost undercuts both orthodox faith and orthodox ritual, not as versions of a central body of truth, but as absolute and exclusive expressions of it. The playful mode of the later poems is itself an expression of the festive spirit of Pentecost. The mixed diction, which so often calls our attention to underlying connections between words from different linguistic universes, makes us aware of translation as a metaphor for all sorts of communication.

The poem that most fully expresses these several aspects of Pentecost is "Whitsunday in Kirchstetten" (*ATH*, p. 82; *SP*, p. 215). The title, which links an Anglican festival and an Austrian place (both of which we can rather quickly translate into component parts), is the first example of the mixture of languages. The epigram (*"Grace dances. I would pipe. Dance ye all.—Acts of John"*), a translation, is another. Almost every phrase of the poem coordinates different languages, levels of diction, customs, or rituals:

> *Komm Schöpfer Geist* I bellow as Herr Beer
> picks up our slim offerings and Pfarrer Lustkandl
>   quietly gets on with the Sacrifice
> as Rome does it: outside car-worshipers enact
>   the ritual exodus from Vienna
> their successful cult demands (though reckoning time
>   by the Jewish week and the Christian year
> like their pedestrian fathers).
>
> [ATH, p. 82; SP, pp. 215–216]

Rome and Canterbury and Vienna, English and German, the city and the country, the Ost-Mark and the dollar, Western and Eastern Europe, car-worshipers and churchgoers, church Latin and "vulgar" German, Christian year and Jewish week:

all are brought together by the image of many tongues speaking one truth, each equally valid and equally invalid.

The meaning is translated into more purely linguistic terms in the next verse paragraph:

> Rejoice: we who were born
>   congenitally deaf are able
> to listen now to rank outsiders. The Holy Ghost
>   does not abhor a golfer's jargon,
> a Lower-Austrian accent, the cadences even
>   of my own little Anglo-American
> musico-literary set (though difficult,
>   saints at least may think in algebra
> without sin): but no sacred nonsense can stand Him.
>
> [*ATH*, p. 83; *SP*, p. 216]

Every hyphenation, every juxtaposition, every pun is a fresh example of the marvel. The easy conversational manner touches each example of unified diversity, and celebrates what is for Auden the central truth that, because the *Schöpfer Geist* does in fact come, one appropriately speaks of God

> . . . with a vocabulary
> made wholesomely profane, open in lexicons
>   to our foes to translate, that we endeavor
> each in his idiom to express the true *magnalia*
>   which need no hallowing from us, loaning terms,
> exchanging graves and legends.
>
> [*ATH*, p. 83; *SP*, pp. 216–217]

Word play becomes Pentecostal celebration, and yet the ultimate mystery remains mysterious:

> There is no Queen's English
> in any context for *Geist* or *Esprit:* about
>   catastrophe or how to behave in one

> I know nothing, except what everyone knows—
>   if there when Grace dances, I should dance.
>   [*ATH*, p. 84; *SP*, p. 217]

Language, syntax, and form create an interplay that locates man in his multiple relations and maps the salients of that location. All the trivial details of place names and idle asides and local custom are parts of the controlling design and of the Pentecostal map, which spreads wider and wider, to Africa and the Bering Sea, without ever abandoning either the central image of the descent of Grace or the specific sense of a day in a small Austrian town. The carefully selected trivia, in effect, demonstrate that Grace does in fact redeem, for, in Auden's theology, perhaps the most important result of the descent of the Spirit is a redemption of trivia that does not alter their triviality. The references to music throughout "Whitsunday in Kirchstetten" make us think of the poem's own created harmonies; all the vulgar details and side routes, the poem suggests, are part of an encompassing design.

There is no set pattern to the late odes, because the rule is that the details should, as in the poems discussed, evolve into a design appropriate to the occasion. Following this process is, in fact, an essential part of the reading of each poem; and, usually, the human is at the center of the map, just as, for Auden, Pentecost is ultimately a celebration of manhood and human scale and the variety of human languages and dialects. The Horatian ode is an ideal vehicle for this celebration. The way in which it holds words in a pattern allows for those incessant acts of translation that represent at once Auden's most obsessive verbal habit and a very specific image of Grace. The play of diction in these poems is metaphorically and sometimes literally macaronic; it is also a recreation of the Pentecostal marvel, a sign of the religious quality and equality of all idioms, of golfer's jargon and musico-literary cadences, and even of scientific euphemisms. At the same time, the lapidary form of the odes celebrates finitude and demonstrates man's ability to fashion with care. And, lauding the things of this earth in their particularity, these poems point us toward our surrounds, both the phenomenal world that is "really there" and the man-made world through which we express our humanity. Finally, the low-keyed meditative tones are expressions of the most distinctive human act, speech that is not noise.

Auden returns to his Pentecostal theme once again in "Prologue at Sixty" (*CWW*, p. 117; *SP*, p. 228):

> Can Sixty make sense to Sixteen-Plus?
> What has my camp in common with theirs,
> with buttons and beards and Be-Ins?
> Much, I hope. In *Acts* it is written
> Taste was no problem at Pentecost.
>
> [*CWW*, pp. 120–121; *SP*, p. 232]

Taste was no problem at Pentecost because that event broke the barriers among classes, nationalities, languages, and orthodoxies; importantly for the poet, it did so in a specifically verbal manner. Auden can and does honor the divisions we receive from Terminus, but he also celebrates those festival acts of translation that cross the boundaries. There is no contradiction here; there is, in fact, a dependency. Auden does not say that Pentecost erased the divisions based on language or established a universal language. It had the opposite effect, that of recognizing differences but also showing the way to coordinate them.

The acts of translation occur in "Prologue at Sixty" along several tangents. In the opening stanzas, by showing man as a complex creature, Auden begins a characteristic route toward identifying the specifically human:

> All but the youngest of the yawning mammals,
> Name-Giver, Ghost-Fearer,
> maker of wars and wisecracks,
> a rum creature, in a crisis always,
> the anxious species to which I belong.
>
> [*CWW*, pp. 117–118; *SP*, p. 229]

Auden's Linnaean method and his comic rhetoric are perfectly matched. The kenning "Name-Giver" is presented as an act of name-giving. The zeugma, "maker of wars and wisecracks," is a wisecrack, and also definitive: man is the only creature who makes either. He is a "rum creature": the only creature who makes and drinks rum, an excellent creature, and a peculiar one; he is always in a crisis, a crisis of time, as suggested by the inversion of crisis and always. And he is anxious in the sense of impatient and in a more clinical sense as well.

He is a multiple creature also in his historical heritage:

> But the Gospel reached the unroman lands.
> I can translate what onion-towers
> of five parish churches preach in Baroque:
> *to make One, there must be Two,*
> *Love is substantial, all Luck is good.*
>
> [*CWW*, p. 118; *SP*, p. 229]

The language of the "code" is loaded; each phrase is a distillation of a basic idea. Unity and multiplicity are interdependent; "Love is substantial" states the meaning of the Incarnation; the word, which is Love, becomes flesh; all luck is good in the sense that luck is a breach in the wall of necessity and thus an instance of human freedom.

This set of paradoxes unites with the Greek Code to form a larger union. In that code

> *a Mind of Honor must acknowledge*
> *the happy eachness of all things,*
> *distinguish even from odd numbers,*
> *and bear witness to what-is-the-case.*

[*CWW*, p. 118; *SP*, p. 230]

Even as the Spirit in its freedom seeks to reverse the fall into time, so man blesses the world in which he lives. Man lives in a world worth celebrating for its own sake, even though it is at the same time properly described by the myth of the Fall.

The presentations of these codes are acts of translation, becoming metaphorically a defense of poetry. All poetry is an act of translation, at once the gift of the Holy Spirit, the theological basis of the poet's art, and the sign of personal speech and hence of love. Auden's poetics is a gospel poetics, a poetics of joy, good news, and festivity; it is other things as well, but its gospel aspect is immensely important. The gospel is for Auden the good news of the redeeming power of love: man exists as a free being in time with both the possibility and the obligation of redeeming time, not by obeying a set of commandments but by accepting the one freeing and overriding commandment to love. This principle, I believe, is partly a matter of temperament—it is certainly apparent in the poems of the thirties—but it receives support from theology. More important is the verbal form Auden finds to express this gospel spirit: the Pentecostal odes are among its finest and fullest expressions.

The ode is not, however, the only form suited to these general purposes. "Ode" is a term for "song," one that suggests a distinction that Horace, for example, did not make. Before considering the even more elaborate arrangements of materials —the three late series of poems that are among Auden's most substantial achievements—I would like to look briefly at the art of arrangement as it appears in two short lyrics.

The song "Deftly, admiral, cast your fly" (*CSP*, p. 271; *SP*, p. 119), is, both in substance and manner, built around the opening adverb. Each stanza presents a different instance of deftness, which comes to stand for human art in a broad sense, poised against the inevitable defeat of that which is human by impersonal, artless forces; each stanza presents an example of human art. What makes the poem successful is the intricacy with which its equipoises are established and maintained— and not, as John Bayley suggests, any affinities with the novel.[14]

> Deftly, admiral, cast your fly
>   Into the slow deep hover,
> Till the wise old trout mistake and die;
>   Salt are the deeps that cover
>   The glittering fleets you led,
>   White is your head.   [*CSP*, p. 271; *SP*, p. 119]

The admiral's past grandeur as leader of a fleet is set against his present small scale triumph over the trout, a smaller but ironically similar conquest. The arts of war and of fly casting are brought together; the wisdom of the admiral is poised against that of the trout, the salt deeps against "the slow deep hover." The quiet but fastidious surface is a triumph of phrasing and rhythm: the words are plain, the simple imperative and declarative forms are bare of ornamentation, the movement of the verse slow. All is controlled; the only hints of disturbance—in the words "hover" and "deeps," in the intransi-

14. See *Romantic Survival*, pp. 37–39.

tive use of "mistake," and the adjectival use of "salt"—are light touches that add to the overriding effect of deftness even as they hint, but only obliquely, at the ferocity of inhuman forces.

The second stanza is both parallel and antithetical to the first:

> Read on, ambassador, engrossed
>   In your favourite Stendhal;
> The Outer Provinces are lost,
>   Unshaven horsemen swill
>   The great wines of the Chateaux
>   Where you danced long ago.   [CSP, p. 271; SP, p. 119]

The great wines, the dancing, and the Stendhal suggest both the elegant life of the diplomat and the life of passion, as if there were in fact an affiliation of the ambassador with the "unshaven horsemen": wines are the emblem both of fine taste and of barbarian revelry (drinking unmixed wine); Stendhal's novels are both high literature and handbooks of passionate selfhood. The poem is so constructed as to suggest the ease with which the balance between these connected antitheses can be tipped one way or the other. For the moment, in the poem, the balance is perfect.

In the third and fourth stanzas the balancing is continued with, presumably, the children of the admiral and the ambassador, totally still though embracing, standing where the properties abut:

> Do not turn, do not lift your eyes
>   Toward the still pair standing
> On the bridge between your properties,
>   Indifferent to your minding:
>   In its glory, in its power,
>   This is their hour.

Nothing your strength, your skill, could do
    Can alter their embrace
Or dispersuade the Furies who
    At the appointed place
    With claw and dreadful brow
       Wait for them now.   [*CSP*, p. 271; *SP*, p. 119]

In the first of these stanzas the productive force of life is balanced by the implicitly destructive force of time; against both are poised the equivalent forces of ambassadorial art and naval strength, each balancing the other and each balanced by the current uses to which the skill and strength are put, with an implicit contrast of past and present. The syntax, with its anaphoras, epanados, and zeugma, maintains the balance. And the balance is not simply rhetorical: strength and skill, the glory and the power, refer to the substance of the poem, to the admiral and the ambassador and what they represent. Finally, the impeccable surface of the poem and its slow careful movement are themselves poised against both the great destructive and the great productive forces.

Auden remarks, in several places, that civilization is "a precarious balance between what Professor Whitehead has called barbaric vagueness and trivial order"; [15] this might well serve as the gloss to the song. The admiral and the ambassador are on the verge of trivial order, trivial contrasted to their past exploits as well as to the young lovers; in the final stanza, all "art," this poem itself, is balanced against "the Furies." Lurking throughout the poem, with appropriate ambiguity, are hints of "barbaric vagueness": the salt deeps, the horsemen, the "claw and dreadful brow" of the Furies. It is triumphant in the deftness of its internal balancing at all levels of subject,

15. See, for example, *The Portable Greek Reader*, ed. W. H. Auden (New York: Viking, 1948), p. 7.

texture, and structure; the final act of balancing is that so apparently slight a poem can serve as the vehicle of so large a subject, for a discussion of the nature of civilization.

The formal pattern of "Deftly, admiral" creates a kind of zone in which words interact, revealing the connections and ironies of the subject. Juxtapositions multiply as each stanza is read; the poem is like four "stills" allowed to create a symmetry of asymmetries. Apart from those internal poises noted, there are larger formal balances: admiral and ambassador against the young lovers; age against youth for all four; art against nature; civilization against too much or too little order. The balance is precarious, but it is there. As I read the poem, it does not say that the gestures of the admiral and ambassador or of the lovers are, in the face of the large forces they oppose, ridiculous (this is Bayley's reading); formally at least, they seem to work. The deft fly casting seems not only a decorous action and a comical avocation for a retired great admiral, but a substantial act of opposition. Stendhal balances the horsemen and the young lovers in the same way. The intricate assemblage of the poem is itself a miracle of balance, like a well-used teeter-totter, a light weight that balances a heavy one by virtue of the artful and exact distribution of its weight. It is a song, a consciously light piece of verse that nonetheless obliquely discusses the nature of civilization, which itself depends on a carefully exercised lightness. It praises and exemplifies art—even fly casting and retirement reading—as an expression of humanism, exalting the civil against too much and too little order.

"The Willow-Wren and the Stare" (*CSP*, p. 272; *SP*, p. 138) presents the relations between man's creatureliness and his spirit in the form of an animal débat. It has a mirroring effect, the result of using the starling and the willow-wren as commentators on the relation between the creaturely and the spiritual in human beings and of making the willow-wren the defender of a "spiritual" view of love that the humans are to some extent contradicting. Ordinarily, in such poems, we suspend our disbelief and do not say, birds can't talk, much less theologize. Here, we suspend it to listen to their words, but the poem reminds us that they *are* birds, as a way of showing us that human love exists somewhere between the purely bodily and the godly. The lovers' speeches and actions concern the relation between their existences as natural and as historical beings, as *homo sapiens* and *homo ludens*, as biological creatures whose bodies are love's agents and as talking creatures who try to disclose themselves to each other in speech; the use of talking birds refracts this doubleness with irony and precision. Talking birds further remind us of the difference between animal noises and human speech: men are capable of lying, animals are not. Here, the hyperbolic speech of the lover—

> 'Dearest of my dear,
> More lively than these waters chortling
>   As they leap the dam,
> My sweetest duck, my precious goose,
>   My white lascivious lamb'   [*CSP*, p. 272; *SP*, p. 138]

—contrasts with the laconic, honest style of the birds; that the lover uses comparisons with animals as he addresses his human lover further complicates and at the same time sharpens the distinctions between human and animal.

Like so many of Auden's poems, "The Willow-Wren and the Stare" is firmly based on a prosaic truth, presented, however, as neither a logical argument nor a dramatized experience. To describe its effects in abstract terms, however, is mis-

leading; the comic poises make their points in their own ways
and the tone is ultimately indescribable:

> 'Hark! Wild Robin winds his horn
>   And, as his notes require,
> Now our laughter-loving spirits
>   Must in awe retire
> And let their kinder partners,
>   Speechless with desire,
> Go in their holy selfishness,
>   Unfunny to the fire.'
> Smiling, silently she threw
>   Her arms about him there:
> *Is it only that?* said the willow-wren;
>   *It's that as well*, said the stare.

[*CSP*, p. 273; *SP*, pp. 138–139]

The lover's speech is a perfect balance of comic awareness.
The final phrase—"it's that as well"—states exactly the relation of "laughter-loving spirits" to "kinder partners": love is
both, it is a conjunction of the spiritual and the creaturely,
and only a complexly playful art can describe it. Here the art
defines, among other things, the exact state of our uncertainty.

I have in mind two images, the crossword puzzle and the
geological-zoological cross section, for Auden's art of arrangement. Auden uses form to create a picture of man in
relation to his environment and to the various parts of his being, especially as represented by other creatures, and the forms
create cross patterns of words, often riddling, mixed in source
and connotation, interacting to suggest a variety of relations.
That the poems also enact human disclosure in its fullest sense
is perhaps the major source of the attention they command.

These images may also serve to characterize the three long
series of poems written during the last two decades. Each of

these works centers on a crucial aspect of man: *Bucolics*, on man the creature; *Horae Canonicae*, on man the agent; and *Thanksgiving for a Habitat*, on man the maker. The three have in common a use of form in which the relationships among poems are much like those among smaller elements in the shorter poems. Each of the three series uses form in a manner appropriate to its intentions. Each is, in its own way, a comprehensive view of the nature of man's existence in the world. Taken together, they represent a large part of Auden's claim to recognition as a major poet. To grasp the complexity of Auden's view of man's place and the fecundity of his craft as it is used to define that place, we must examine each of these works in detail.

4. *The Early History of Late Man*

The poems in *Bucolics*, first published as a group in 1955,[1] have been praised both individually and collectively. Several questions, however, still need to be asked about them. Is there an underlying design to the series, or is it simply a loose grouping of poems on a common, general theme? Does the title simply indicate a general interest in man and nature, or are there more fundamental senses in which the poems are versions of pastoral? Do they address themselves to the questions concerning man's nature that are implicit in the pastoral mode? I wish to suggest that the poems have an underlying design best understood as a sophisticated realization of a pastoral vision, and touch on the most serious issues raised by the pastoral mode. Auden's use of the mode tells us much about how a modern poet uses, modifies, and extends an inherited tradition and set of conventions.

The series collects in a new arrangement a number of di-

1. The series first appeared as a whole in the recording *W. H. Auden Reading His Poems* (New York: Caedmon Publishers, 1954; recording TC 1019). According to Spears, the recording was made December 12, 1953; see *Auden*, p. 311. "Woods," the first individual poem to appear, was published in *The Listener*, 11 Dec. 1952, p. 974. The short period between first serial publication and the recording of the whole series supports the notion that the series was composed not as a loose collection but as an organized whole.

verse threads from Auden's earlier poetry and thought. In part, the poems present themselves as landscapes. There are two primary senses of that term: the artistic portrayal of a natural scene, and the natural scene that is portrayed. Between these, there are, for Auden, several specialized meanings. There is the "inner space" referred to in *New Year Letter*, where the language of sovereignty and real estate suggests a private garden, planted, cultivated, and ruled over by the self:

> The landscape of his will and need
> Where he is sovereign indeed,
> The state created by his acts
> Where he patrols the forest tracts
> Planted in childhood . . .   [*CLP*, p. 111]

Auden also uses a more insistently psychic, less fancifully allegorical sense of landscape. In the "Seven Stages" section of *The Age of Anxiety*, he describes what "many people reveal in a state of semi-intoxication": "So it was now as they sought that state of prehistoric happiness which, by human beings, can only be imagined in terms of a landscape bearing a symbolic resemblance to the human body" (*CLP*, p. 296). This notion of landscape—or dreamscape—becomes, in *The Age of Anxiety*, fairly complicated. The characters go through a series of imagined psychic landscapes. Each responds with his own personal psychic landscape, presented as a place he remembers "because something important happened there." Finally the poem moves toward a communal landscape of archetypal images. It portrays a quest for a replica of paradise, for a landscape that can image community and human love. In *The Age of Anxiety* it is not clear whether or not the quest is futile, unsuccessful, and/or foolish. To complicate matters, the four characters questing through individual landscapes correspond in part to the four Jungian faculties of man.[2] Hence not only each individual but also the various faculties of every person have unique representative landscapes capable of integration into a communal and allegorical whole. As in "In Praise of Limestone," a landscape at once paradisiacal and childish is presented as a positive image of our longing for Edenic wholeness and of love.

Auden also uses landscape as a way of representing human emotions in terms of external reality: "While Shakespeare, for example, thought of the non-human world in terms of the human, Rilke thinks of the human in terms of the non-human, of what he calls Things (Dinge). . . . Thus, one of Rilke's more characteristic devices is the expression of human life in terms of landscape." [3] We recognize this practice as the basis of many of Auden's figures of speech (e.g., "desert of the heart"). The device, however, is a complex one. In "On This Island," which is both a landscape and a seascape, the interaction of the human and the physical figures for the landscape is itself tropaic for the interaction of man and nature. Similarly, the lines from the Yeats elegy—"And the seas of pity lie / Locked and frozen in each eye"—go beyond the simple expression of the human emotion ("pity") in nonhuman terms ("seas"). They use an image of a human solvent ("tears") that achieves the unlocking and unfreezing of the nonhuman terms and thus not only coordinates but also resolves the opposition of the human and nonhuman.

The use of the term "Dinge," in the discussion of Rilke, introduces another aspect of Auden's use of landscape, one

2. See Edward Callan, "Allegory in Auden's *The Age of Anxiety*," *Twentieth Century Literature*, 10 (1965), 155–165.

3. "Rilke in English," *New Republic*, 100 (6 Sept. 1939), 135.

that becomes increasingly important in the later poems. When, in *New Year Letter*, Auden talks of "RILKE whom *die Dinge* bless," he suggests an animation in things of nature, and more and more he has talked of the blessedness of things, all things (as in "Precious Five," with its injunction to *"Bless what there is for being"*). Among the deleterious effects of modern science, Auden has said, are the "loss of belief in the eternity of the physical universe," "the loss of belief in the significance and reality of sensory phenomena," and, especially, the loss of "the traditional conception of the phenomenal world" as "one of sacramental analogies" (*DH*, p. 78). Hence, if Auden's use of landscape involves the humanizing of nature, part of it also involves the reassertion that nature is worth our unqualified blessing and capable of giving us *its* blessings.

Besides being a series of landscapes, *Bucolics* has a basic and persistent concern with questions of man as an evolved and evolving creature. Early, Auden identified the force of evolution with human love and, at times, the revolutionary spirit. A person or class useless to further evolution, he believed, virtually cooperated with the death wish, which Freud defines as the desire to return to an earlier stage of evolutionary development. In "Venus Will Now Say a Few Words," the force of evolution, wittily defined in the title from *Collected Poetry* of 1945 as Venus, patiently explains to someone useless to further evolution just how the system works:

> To reach that shape for your face to assume,
> Pleasure to many and despair to some,
> I shifted ranges, lived epochs handicapped
> By climate, wars, or what the young men kept,
> Modified theories on the types of dross,
> Altered desire and history of dress.   [*CSP*, p. 33]

Randall Jarrell accurately summarizes the evolutionism of the early poems:

> Auden relates science to Marxism in an unexpected but perfectly orthodox way: Lenin says somewhere that in the most general sense Marxism is a theory of evolution. Auden quite consciously makes this connection; evolution, as a source both of insight and image, is always just at the back of his earliest poems. . . . IV in *Poems* ["A Free One," *CSP*, p. 29] is nothing but an account of evolution—by some neo-Hardyish *I* behind it—and a rather Marxist extension of it into man's history and everyday life.[4]

We recognize in the early poems the beginnings of a continuing effort to coordinate notions of man as an organism obeying laws of nature and a member of society obeying laws of history and to bring together different kinds of knowledge to present a full picture of man. Jarrell believed that Auden later abandoned this "tough" evolutionism in favor of a "soft" Christian view, and that, when he did so, the language of his poetry in turn lost *its* toughness. I think *Bucolics* shows Jarrell to have been wrong on both counts, but, in any case, Auden never lost his teleological cast of mind, his fundamental curiosity about how things developed or are developing, and he has not ceased attempting to correlate ontogenic growth with phylogenic, psychic with societal, biological with historical. *The Age of Anxiety* represents a large scale attempt to view human development as an evolutionary process. The distance from saying "In my veins there is . . . a memory of a fish"— that is, that we recall earlier stages of evolutionary development, that Hegel's law operates psychologically—to saying that there is in every person a memory of paradisiacal com-

4. "Changes of Attitude and Rhetoric in Auden's Poetry," *Southern Review*, 7 (1941), 328–329.

pleteness is not as great as Jarrell, Beach, and others who see severe changes in Auden's basic intellectual orientation believe.

By its title, *Bucolics* claims kinship with a complicated literary tradition. The pastoral mode involves the sophisticated adoption of a conventionalized innocence, and thus creates a complex interplay between artifice and simplicity. As a long-developing tradition, it carries with it considerable luggage of conventionalized attitudes and techniques, and yet it is always applied to defining the simple, natural, and unadorned; every new use of the tradition both restates the element of simplicity and adds to the accumulation of convention.

Teasing combinations of simplicity and high artifice are so general and pervasive in Auden's work as to need little mention. He has always been interested in "worlds imaginary, but real" (to use his characterization of Tolkien's works), in "secondary worlds." A characteristic pattern of his work is that of going into a world of fantasy and illusion to discover "where we really are," just as, in *The Sea and the Mirror*, a set of multiple actions is based on the original pattern from *The Tempest* of the courtly parties going into the half-natural, half-artificial world of the enchanted island to discover the "actual" relationships usable and desirable in the courtly world.

The pattern takes many forms. Going elsewhere is a way of simplifying and unifying the tangled relations existing at the point of embarkation and finally showing that there is no real place other than "here," where we are, and no other time than "now," the time being. We go into unreality, seek "a change of air" or take a trip, to discover who we really are, what our place really is. In "Whither?" (*CSP*, p. 119) the pattern is dramatized as totally relative motion; we do not know what is fixed and what is moving. The pattern exists in most of Auden's quest and journey poems, with the journey usually figured as both voyage out and voyage home, the Good Place a false hope, an attractive possibility, and a point of perspective, just as Arden Forest is both more and less real than the court of Duke Frederick, existence in it both a masking and an unmasking, the journey both an escape and a confrontation.

Pastoral brings all these concerns into a complex artistic form, but the central question concerns the meaning of the word *natural*. For Auden, this question demands that particular attention be given to man's simultaneous existence in and out of nature, as a being who has evolved out of a purely natural existence and who no longer directly *perceives* himself as such a creature (since the immediate data of his consciousness are those of his existential freedom as a historical being) yet at the same time *knows* that he is a natural being. Paradoxically, perhaps, the further he "evolves" away from nature, the more he discovers that both he and the natural world are evolving things and that their evolutionary stories are interdependent. At an advanced state *of* evolution, man begins to be able *to trace* evolution. Thus, just as the light, playful, and at times apparently frivolous manner of *Bucolics* is akin to the pastoral mode, so also is their serious attention to man's nature and his art.

It is possible to identify specifically at least one source of the ideas and language of *Bucolics*. The first stanza of the second poem, "Woods," reads as follows:

> Sylvan meant savage in those primal woods
> Piero di Cosimo so loved to draw,
> Where nudes, bears, lions, sows with women's heads,
> Mounted and murdered and ate each other raw,

Nor thought the lightning-kindled bush to tame
But, flabbergasted, fled the useful flame.

[*CSP*, p. 257; *SP*, p. 145]

The stanza clearly echoes several passages from Erwin Panofsky's essay, "The Early History of Man in Two Cycles of Paintings by Piero di Cosimo," especially one in which Panofsky discusses Piero the man:

But one of Vasari's expressions furnishes a key to the nature of the man: '*si contentava di veder salvatico ogni cosa, come la sua natura.*' This word *salvatico*, derived from *silva* like our 'savage,' explains in a flash both Piero's obsession with primitivistic notions and his magic power in bringing them to life by his brush.

Earlier, Panofsky quotes Boccaccio, who, to demonstrate that Vulcan is the "very founder of human civilization," quotes Vitruvius' account of the origins of building:

'In the olden days men were born like wild beasts in woods and caves and groves, and kept alive by eating raw food. Somewhere, meanwhile, the close-grown trees, tossed by storms and winds, and rubbing their branches together, caught fire. Terrified by the flames, those who were near the spot fled.'

Later in the essay, discussing two Pieros in the Metropolitan Museum in New York, "Hunting Scene" and "Return from the Hunt," Panofsky says:

As there is no real separation between mankind and animals on the one hand, mankind and half-beasts such as satyrs and centaurs on the other, all these creatures love and mate, or fight and kill, indiscriminately, without paying any attention whatever to their common enemy, the forest fire. . . . [It is] a jungle fight of all against all (for instance, a lion attacking a bear but at the same time being attacked by a man).

And, discussing still another Piero, "Landscape with Animals," he notes:

The woods are still haunted by the strange creatures which resulted from the promiscuous mating of men and animals, for the sow with the face of a woman and the goat with the face of a man are by no means Bosch-like phantasms. . . . These strange creatures seem peacefully to share the woods and fields with lions, deer, cranes, cows, and an enticing family of bears. . . . [But] these beasts and half-beasts are not so much peaceful as exhausted by flight and stunned by terror of the forest fire. Man, too, is now aware of this fire, but instead of being frightened he seizes his chance to catch some of the cows and oxen that have fled from the burning woods; their future yoke he carries providently on his shoulder.[5]

It should be clear that when Auden wrote *Bucolics* he was not only aware of the Panofsky essay but very thoroughly acquainted with it: the language of the first stanza of "Woods" is a thorough mixture of the language of several different passages from the essay. Indeed, the texture of the stanza, with its scrambled images and actions, recreates the quality both of the paintings referred to and of Panofsky's descriptions of them.

"Influences," "sources," and "echoes" are tricky matters in Auden's poetry. Even when we have established that Auden knew at a particular time a given source, we can never with complete assurance establish a connection between general views in the source and general views in Auden's work. Everything we know about Auden suggests that his habit is to

5. *Studies in Iconology: Humanistic Themes in the Art of the Renaissance*, 2d ed. (NewYork: Harper, 1967), pp. 66–67, 39, 53–54, 55; 1st publ., 1939. Miss Janice Carlisle called my attention to this source.

refashion materials from "sources" to make them serve his own purpose. Auden's critics have often confused a name with a field of interest; for instance, Freudianism, Marxism, or Darwinism with interest in psychology, society, or evolution. Nonetheless, with these caveats in mind, I would like to suggest that Panofsky's essay indicates much about the themes, methods, and structure not only of "Woods," but also of the whole of *Bucolics*. To demonstrate this point, it is necessary to return to the essay.

Panofsky attempts, primarily by iconographical identification and analysis, to establish the thematic unity of two groups of superficially unrelated Pieros, as

one comprehensive cycle which, in a rich and persuasive manner, would have represented the two earliest phases of human history as described in classical writing . . . : 'Vulcanus,' raging in the woods, while man, not yet befriended by him, shares the excitements and fears of animals and hybrid monsters; and 'Vulcanus' again, descending upon the earth in human form and pointing the path towards civilization. [p. 57]

Panofsky wants not only to establish thematic connections among the now scattered paintings, but also to argue that the two series were "executed for the same employer" as a grand design for a small anteroom and a grand *salone*, and further to suggest that Piero's much later depictions of Prometheus "might be considered a belated postscript to the Vulcan epic," with Prometheus as a kind of successor to Vulcan, bringing not the physical fire of Vulcan but a celestial light of knowledge, though "at the expense of happiness and peace of mind."

Behind this argument about the composition, arrangement, and mythography of the paintings lies Panofsky's larger concern—more fully developed in his more famous essay, "*Et in*

Arcadia Ego: Poussin and the Elegiac Tradition"—with the humanistic implications of two conflicting notions of the nature of man's early history:

There had been from the very beginning of classical speculation two contrasting opinions about the primeval life of man: The 'soft' or positivistic primitivism as formulated by Hesiod depicted the primitive form of existence as a 'golden age,' in comparison with which the subsequent phases were nothing but successive stages of one prolonged Fall from Grace; whereas the 'hard,' or negativistic, primitivism imagined the primitive form of existence as a truly bestial state, from which mankind had fortunately escaped through technical and intellectual progress.

Both these conceptions were reached by a mental abstraction from civilized life. But while 'soft' primitivism imagines a civilized life cleansed of everything abhorrent and problematic, 'hard' primitivism imagines a civilized life deprived of all comforts and cultural achievements. 'Soft' primitivism idealizes the initial condition of the world, and is therefore in harmony with a religious interpretation of human life and destiny, particularly with the various doctrines of Original Sin. 'Hard' primitivism, on the other hand, sought to be realistic in its reconstruction of the initial state of the world, and therefore fitted nicely into the scheme of a rationalistic, or even materialistic, philosophy. This philosophy imagines the rise of humanity as an entirely natural process, exclusively due to the innate gifts of the human race, whose civilization began with the discovery of fire, all ensuing developments being accounted for in a perfectly logical way.

Piero, as Panofsky presents him, is not a philosopher, but his treatment of images puts him clearly if unconsciously into the camp of the "hard" primitivists. Indeed, part of Panofsky's argument is that Piero, whom Vasari and everyone else thought of as rather an odd fish, so to speak, arrived at a sophisticated evolutionism not through theory but through his own atavistic experiences:

Like Lucretius, Piero conceived of human evolution as a process due to the inborn faculties and talents of the race. . . . But like Lucretius, Piero was sadly aware of the dangers entailed by this development. He joyfully sympathized with the rise of humanity beyond the bestial hardships of the stone age, but he regretted any step beyond the unsophisticated phase which he would have termed the reign of Vulcan and Dionysos. To him civilization meant a realm of beauty and happiness as long as man kept in close contact with Nature, but a nightmare of oppression, ugliness and distress as soon as man became estranged from her.[6]

As in the essay on Poussin, Panofsky concludes that the true Arcadian spirit more closely approximates "hard" primitivism, with its evolutionist and progressive affinities, than it does the "soft" primitivism of sentimental arcadianism.

With this summary of Panofsky's essay in mind, I would suggest that *Bucolics* is closely related to the paintings of Piero as described by Panofsky; that the poems address themselves to questions connected with the categories of "hard" and "soft" primitivism and hence with the relation of art and civilization to man's origins; that the seven poems can be thought of as a grouping similar to that which Panofsky postulates for Piero's paintings. Since the essay is Auden's direct source, it does not really matter whether Panofsky's speculation is right; what matters is only that Auden found it useful. The series is not a narrative of the prehistory and history of man but a series of *paysages moralisés* whose iconography suggests successive stages in man's development: Auden's treatment of images is somewhat similar to Panofsky's treatment of iconography.

Auden's decision to construct iconographic landscapes rather than narrative allegories probably has two origins. One probable source is the apparent failure of *The Age of Anxiety*, which attempts to treat the phylogenic and ontogenic

6. *Studies in Iconology*, pp. 40–41, 65.

history of man both as a series of landscapes and as a series of narratives growing out of a dramatized situation; the work suffers, I think, from a confusion of spatial and temporal form.[7] A more positive source is Auden's long-standing interest in allegorical landscape as a method of presentation, evidenced not only in Auden's reading of such essays as Panofsky's, but also, and more important, in his own superb essay, *The Enchafèd Flood, or, The Romantic Iconography of the Sea,* first delivered as lectures in 1949 and published in 1950.

The speaker of *Bucolics* is not a shepherd; but if we accept as pastoral Marvell's "The Mower against Gardens," we certainly can also accept *Bucolics,* noting that its speaker, with his fine mixture of naiveté and sophistication, is a fair modern rendering of the traditional shepherd-poet. Although the play of language and reference is very much alive to the incongruities between hard and soft primitivism, the poems ultimately use the two "modes" or "concepts" as the components of a multiple perspective on man, whom Auden conceives as both a fallen and an evolved being (fallen insofar as he is a historical and history-making being, evolved insofar as he is a creature). But his status as a historical being can be defined as a part of his evolution, and he now exists with mnemonic traces of both atavistic primitivism and Edenic simplicity. Although there are substantial contradictions between hard and soft primitivism, the contradictions are necessary to define the state of man. The poems are finally as much about art as they are

7. For me, too much happens iconographically to be supported by the narratives and the dramatic situation. Or, perhaps more precisely, to support allegorical expansion through both images and plot one would need a much more complex unit than the alliterative line: a unit, for instance, like the Spenserian stanza, through which each step of narrative can be expanded and analyzed. But I am far from certain *The Age of Anxiety* is a failure.

about nature, but especially about art as a part of the evolutionary development of man and as an instance of those impulses towards speech and making that define man's "fall" into
humanity. Auden, like Piero, might well celebrate Vulcan—
"the only ungentlemanly workman . . . in the Olympian
leisure class" [8]—as he does Hephaestos, Vulcan's Greek prototype.

"Winds," the opening poem, brings together and compares
three acts of creation: of *Homo sapiens*, of civil life, and of
poetry. In the first stanza, we sense both festivity and stateli-
ness, the serious purpose as well as the playful means of the
verbal rites being undertaken:

> Deep, deep below our violences,
> Quite still, lie our First Dad, his watch
>   And many little maids,
> But the boneless winds that blow
>   Round law-court and temple
> Recall to Metropolis
>   That Pliocene Friday when,
> At His holy insufflation
>   (Had he picked a teleost
> Or an arthropod to inspire,
>   Would our death also have come?)
> One bubble-brained creature said;—
>   'I am loved, therefore I am'—:
> And well by now might the lion
>   Be lying down with the kid,
> Had he stuck to that logic.   [*CSP*, p. 255; *SP*, p. 143]

These lines suggest an archaeological find and, at the same
time, a causal relation, as if our violences were connected to
what lies deep below them. The sudden shift in diction, from

8. *Studies in Iconology*, p. 58.

the stately opening to "First Dad," introduces the kind of riddle that dominates the surface of the whole series: First Dad is both Adam and that primate from whom we evolved, a prehistoric ancestor; his watch and the many little maids suggest a primitive burial grounds, the geological strata in which fossils are found, and perhaps also a biological clock and the daughter cells that lead down to, and determine in part, the character of our present existence. In spite of the fact that our origins are buried, hence skeletons, "boneless winds" recall (jiggle the memory, are an image of) those origins. Pliocene Friday is a runic mixture of Darwinian and biblical accounts of creation, compressed in a phrase: Pliocene is the geological age of the evolution of man; Friday, if we use the Christian rather than the Jewish calendar, is the fifth day of creation, the day of man's creation; the hint of Good Friday is appropriate because, as the parenthetical phrase in the middle of the stanza suggests, death is implicit in creation. "Insufflation" continues the mixture of connotations, being a medical practice (one insufflates an organ, like the lungs or the fallopian tubes, by blowing a gas into it to discover patency), a religious ritual (one insufflates holy water to symbolize the presence of the Holy Spirit, a priest breathes on catechumens, presumably as a rite of initiation into belief), and the image of God's creation of man. The play of words telescopes accounts of creation and views of man as a spiritual and biological creature. Far from being an attempt to reconcile points of view, it works like the principle of complementarity: we understand man, necessarily, only if we understand him simultaneously as both spiritual being and biological creature: the word games create the necessary double focus.

The stanza is exactly dissected by the quirkish question that, once again, mixes religious and biological terminology, and further compounds the perspective by the double sense of inspire and the homonymic pun on anthropoid. The question is doubly a riddle: it might mean, had another species been given consciousness, would we know ourselves as dying creatures? It might also mean, had we, the inspired ones, been another species, would we still have been fallen creatures? And there is also the riddle of what the answer to either question is. The bubble-brained creature is the primate who, at the moment of the evolutionary jump, suddenly "fell into consciousness," that is, had a brain capable of attaining self-awareness. He is bubble-brained in the sense of having a small brain, in the slang sense of "stupid," and in the sense, biologically crucial and accurate, of having a hollow brain. Here, as often, Auden disguises a very precise idea by using a flippant term. He follows a line of argument and speculation that occurs in Loren Eiseley's *The Immense Journey*. Eiseley is discussing a crucial link in the evolutionary chain, the Snout, a "fresh-water Crossopterygian":

It is interesting to consider what sort of creatures we, the remote descendants of the Snout, might be, except for that green quagmire out of which he came. Mammalian insects we should have been—solid-brained, our neurones wired for mechanical responses, our lives running out with the perfection of beautiful, intricate, and mindless clocks. . . . The increase was not much. It was two bubbles, two thin-walled little balloons at the end of the Snout's small brain. The cerebral hemispheres had appeared. . . .

The brain was a thin-walled tube. . . . It could only exist as a thing of thin walls permeated with oxygen. . . . The Snout lived on a bubble, two bubbles in his brain.

It was not that his thinking was deep; it was only that it had to be thin. The little bubbles of the hemisphere helped to spread the

area upon which higher correlation centers could be built, and
yet preserve those areas from the disastrous thickenings . .
which culminate in the so-called solid brain. It is the brain of insects, of the modern fishes, of some reptiles and all birds. Always
it marks the appearance of elaborate patterns of instinct and the
end of thought. A road has been taken which, anatomically, is
well-nigh irretraceable; it does not lead in the direction of a high
order of consciousness.

Wherever, instead, the thin sheets of gray matter expand upward into the enormous hemispheres of the human brain, laughter
or it may be sorrow, enters in.[9]

The creature, then, is stupid in a complex sense, although, unlike teleosts (modern fishes) and arthropods (insects, crusta-
ceans, arachnids) he, being bubble-brained, has cerebral hemispheres and thus the potentiality not simply to be smart but to
have consciousness, to be capable of laughter and sorrow, to
be able to know his state, and hence, taking all of these together, to fall from mindless innocence. The creature's logic
both is and is not fallacious. John Fuller suggests it is "a
psuedo-Cartesian argument for self-sufficiency" as in the refer-

9. *The Immense Journey* (London: Victor Gollancz, 1958)
pp. 52–54. This chapter, "The Snout," first appeared in *Harper's*
201 (1950). Auden, in a review of Eiseley's *The Unexpected Universe*
(*The New Yorker*, 21 Feb. 1970, pp. 124–125), states that his first
acquaintance with Eiseley's work was reading *The Immense Journey*
which was first published in 1957; this would seem to rule out a
direct influence on *Bucolics*. But the passage quoted strongly suggests
that Auden had read "The Snout" when he wrote *Bucolics*, athough
there is no direct evidence for this supposition. The important point
is that Auden, from whatever source, had and made use of a very
thorough knowledge of going theories of evolution when writing
Bucolics. I am grateful to Professor Eiseley for answering my queries
about the publication dates of his writings, and thus helping me to
establish which of them Auden could or could not have read at any
given date.

ence to Diaghilev in "September 1, 1939," [10] but the line is perhaps more accurately read as an improvement of the Cartesian formula, with the bubble-brained creature expressing his awareness as an experience of God's love for him—a Cartesian, but neither a Christian nor a biological fallacy. Its accuracy comes from its union of creation, fall, evolutionary leap, and divine "inspiration" in an image of love.

The final lines are also playfully riddling: the reference to Isaiah is mixed since the original biblical reference has the leopard lying down with the kid and the calf and the young lion and the fatling together; the mixture is in keeping with the image of a potential peaceable kingdom. More puzzling is the use of an image of the coming of the Lord as something that might be precipitated by sticking to the logic of love. We quickly see that there is a sense, for Auden, in which redemption is accelerated by following the gospel of love, but there is also a witty point in the formulation: Auden uses the animals of the Bible to figure the peace of redemption, to describe the hypothetical consequences of man's sticking to the logic that marked his emergence from the strictly animal world. Wind serves as an image both of memory (by which we recall our creaturely origins) and of the giving of life. (Precisely, for, as Eiseley points out, the thin membrane of the bubble-brained Snout is what allowed for the development of the cerebral hemispheres and, ultimately, of human consciousness because it allows oxygen—another instance of wind—"to insufflate" the brain.) The sentence traces a journey backward to origins and forward to the possible consequences of following the doctrine of love; its playful dignity, fusing the divine and the human, is thus a figure for the divinity of human creation.

10. *Reader's Guide*, p. 219.

The first stanza suggests the compatibility of several accounts of man's creation; the second suggests that man's worldly goal, "the Authentic City," will also be reached by evolutionary processes:

> (Across what brigs of dread,
> Down what gloomy galleries,
>   Must we stagger or crawl
> Before we may cry—O look!?)   [CSP, p. 255; SP, p. 143]

The third stanza aligns the act of poetry with the other two acts of creation (of man and of the authentic city) and places both the poet and the reader between the origin and the goal. The poet, in a sense, prays that he may celebrate both man's origins and his direction:

> That every verbal rite
>   May be fittingly done,
> And done in anamnesis
>   Of what is excellent
> Yet a visible creature,
>   Earth, Sky, a few dear names.   [CSP, p. 256; SP, p. 144]

That excellent and visible creature is man. Man is an excellent creation, a miraculous one, and yet a creature, a being with a body who is visible to us and subject to biological law, and he is placed between earth and sky, his humanity manifest in his ability to name.

In "The Virgin & The Dynamo" Auden says that "the poet's activity in creating a poem is analogous to God's activity in creating man after his own image":

Every poem . . . is an attempt to present an analogy to that paradisal state in which Freedom and Law, System and Order are united in harmony. Every good poem is very nearly a Utopia. . . . The effect of beauty . . . is good to the degree that, through its analogies, the goodness of created existence, the historical fall into unfreedom and disorder, and the possibility of regaining paradise through repentance and forgiveness are recognized.   [*DH*, pp. 70, 71]

Poetry, in this formulation, is a kind of way station, memorial of prehistory, precursive of redemption, accepting of the inbetweenness of man existing in time. "Winds," by exploring the analogies among the various kinds of creation, focuses attention on questions central to the whole series: the relation of man the creature to man the spiritual being; the bases of civil life; the contribution of poetry to it.

"Woods" contains the specific references to the Pieros that depict man "ante Vulcanum" and "sub Vulcano"; it, too, covers a whole historical development, presented as a series of antitheses between "sylvan" and "savage," between soft and hard primitivism. The woods themselves are a device of perspective. They establish human scale, both in time, since the woods reach back into prehistory and will continue beyond the lifetime of living men, and in space, since they dwarf men. The poem is not so much about woods as about our continuing double attitude toward them, and indicates that there is psychological truth in both the "sylvan" and the "savage" views.

The poem takes the form of an extemporaneous discussion of its subject, an all-purpose description of the features and uses of woods; it makes apparently gratuitous references and takes tangents that, once mentioned, define the basic themes. It continually focuses attention on the way the meanings of words change and interact. The opening line draws attention to lexical changes, and the reference to the scene depicted by Piero suggests a connection between woods and the origin of speech: the fire in the woods brought the "savages" together for warmth, whence, grouped together, they invented speech as a means of mutual understanding. Separated from nature by our powers of speech, we continually return to nature and reinvolve ourselves with it; word play is both the method and, in part, the subject disclosed in the poem.

The playful nature of the poem's surface continually shows the savage within the sylvan:

> Reduced to patches, owned by hunting squires,
> Of villages with ovens and a stocks,
> They whispered still of most unsocial fires.
>
> [*CSP*, p. 257; *SP*, p. 145]

Civilization is not as civil as it thinks, and those savage woods, made sylvan, are owned by squires who hunt. The villages have ovens in which to cook the animals killed: the advance of civilization is to eat meat cooked rather than raw, as in the woods of the first stanza. They also have a stocks, the instrument of a human but inhumane punishment. The woods' whispering "still of most unsocial fires" recalls the use of winds, woods, and fire to represent stages of savagery and civility in Piero's woods. And the last three lines of the stanza specifically mock "soft" pastoral, by juxtaposing the synecdochical "Crown and Mitre" against the meiotic "silly flocks," by the play on the archaic ("worthy") and modern ("foolish") senses of "silly," and by the intentionally bad, but still revealing, pun on "flocks" (the "Mitre" warns its "flocks" to approve "the pasture's humdrum rhythms"). The reversals of meaning, the canny misuses, and the mocking metaphors work back to the central formulation: man is a natural creature who transcends, but never abandons, his natural origins. Every time he returns to nature, whether for a picnic or a pastoral poem, he replays the drama of his evolution.

Among the contrasts "Woods" develops are several between the noises of nature and the words of man:

> Old sounds re-educate an ear grown coarse,
> As Pan's green father suddenly raps out
> A burst of undecipherable Morse,
> And cuckoos mock in Welsh, and doves create
> In rustic English over all they do
> To rear their modern family of two.
>
> [*CSP*, p. 258; *SP*, p. 146]

The whimsical translation of bird sounds into language not quite understandable (Morse Code, Welsh, rustic English) is exactly what birds cannot accomplish. That natural creatures cannot but that men can and want to turn their noise into something that can be deciphered indicates the gap between us and even this highly domesticated instance of nature. Man's various interpretations of the meaning of woods are a definition of his position in and out of nature.

The final lines maintain the double focus:

> A small grove massacred to the last ash,
> An oak with heart-rot, give away the show:
> This great society is going smash.   [*CSP*, p. 258; *SP*, p. 146]

"This great society" recalls Auden's distinction among kinds of "pluralities": crowds, societies, and communities. Crowds are something that men are always in danger of degenerating into, a purely arithmetic collection of things; communities, "n members united, to use a definition of Saint Augustine's, by a common love of something other than themselves" (*DH*, p. 64), are something that only men can achieve. Less likely than men to become a crowd, incapable of becoming a community, the woods, a great society, again serve to define what is human. The last line— "A culture is no better than its woods"—can mean two things: a culture is to be judged by how it tends its woods, and a culture, like a woods, is subject to laws of decay. Here as at the beginning, "Woods" suggests an easy commerce between man and woods, humans and nature, and woods viewed as sylvan and woods viewed as savage. It also represents a point in man's history at which his separateness from nature does not entail total separation.

"Mountains," both the poem and the image, suggests much sharper divisions between natural and civil man and between man and nature than either of the first two poems. Like the solid, craggy stanza form, and like the mountains themselves, the poem builds an image of a severe hiatus between civil and precivil man. The poem takes us into the mountains, and, iconographically, back to ages of ice, stone, and bronze:

> Tunnels begin, red farms disappear,
>   Hedges turn to walls,
> Cows become sheep, you smell peat or pinewood, you hear
>   Your first waterfalls,
>
> And what looked like a wall turns out to be a world
>   With measurements of its own
> And a style of gossip. To manage the Flesh,
>   When angels of ice and stone
> Stand over her day and night who make it so plain
> They detest any kind of growth, does not encourage
> Euphemisms for the effort: here wayside crucifixes
>   Bear witness to a physical outrage,
>   And serenades too
> Stick to bare fact; 'O my girl has a goitre,
>   I've a hole in my shoe!'
>
> Dour. Still, a fine refuge. That boy behind his goats
>   Has the round skull of a clan

That fled with bronze before a tougher metal.

[*CSP*, pp. 259–260; *SP*, pp. 147–148]

The series has moved forward in two senses: the reference in "Mountains" to the Bronze Age indicates a stage in man's early history later than that at the beginning of "Woods"; and the degree of division, the sharpness of the split between civil man and natural man (an internal as well as an external split), has increased. The images of the natural world are more foreboding: "perfect monsters—remember Dracula— / Are bred on crags in castles"; even mountain climbers "are a bit alarming." But the images of civil man are also altered. The poem is full of phrases that suggest an effete civility—"a retired dentist who only paints mountains," "Well, I won't," "I'm nordic myself"—which fully emerges in the final stanza:

> To be sitting in privacy, like a cat
>   On the warm roof of a loft,
> Where the high-spirited son of some gloomy tarn
>   Comes sprinting down through a green croft,
> Bright with flowers laid out in exquisite splodges
> Like a Chinese poem, while, near enough, a real darling
> Is cooking a delicious lunch . . .   [*CSP*, p. 260; *SP*, p. 148]

The language transforms the mountains from the gothic into the precious; the tough, "dour," noneuphemistic style gives way to terms like "exquisite," "delicious," "darling." Mountains, then, come to represent a severity of separation of man and nature and of natural and civil man that turns the human into cloying and the natural into ominous.

The first three poems form a subgroup depicting two parallel movements, from creation to Stone Age, from a balance of Eden, the world, and Paradise, to a comic imbalance, and then to a still comic but slightly ominous separation. The next two poems, "Lakes" and "Islands," are linked as mirror images ("What is cosier than the shore / Of a lake turned inside out?") and show two sides of civil man as well as two further, much later, stages in man's history.

"Lakes," at the center of the cycle, portrays a highly civilized coordination of human and nonhuman scale:

> A lake allows an average father, walking slowly,
>   To circumvent it in an afternoon,
> And any healthy mother to halloo the children
>   Back to her bedtime from their games across.
>   [*CSP*, p. 260; *SP*, p. 149]

The size of lakes is defined by the rituals and schedules of family life, well regulated in accord with freedom and order: the father's pace and the mother's halloo define a balance of human scale and natural scale. Although the art does not advertise itself, the locutions, the control of vocabulary, the accumulation of images, and the modulations of tone are immensely skilful. The lake "allows" ("is large and small enough" and "permits") like a benign monarch. The father is "average" in the senses of "statistical mean" and "ordinary." The whole clause is a small triumph of phrasing—the precision of usage, so neatly expressing size and motion, is a lexical trope for the orderly view of nature "lakes" represent. The mother's healthy voice, bringing the children from *their* games to *her* bedtime, coordinates the lake's breadth and the human voice with a gracious balance of freedom and discipline, of nature and man.

Out of the deceptively homely descriptions emerge the images of the circle and the cross-lake dialogue as emblems of a proper relation between the patterns of life and the order of nature. These images are then extended. In the second stanza, "A month in a lacustrine atmosphere / Would find the fluvial rivals waltzing not exchanging / . . . rhyming insults." In the third, "pensive chiefs" of Christianity converge, "making catholic the figure / Of three small fishes in a triangle." And in the fourth,

> Sly Foreign Ministers should always meet beside one,
>   For, whether they walk widdershins or deasil,
> The path will yoke their shoulders to one liquid centre
>   Like two old donkeys pumping as they plod.
>
> [*CSP*, p. 261; *SP*, p. 149]

The image is double: as man is brought into harmony with nature, he opens up the possibility of harmony with other men, and "sly Foreign Ministers" can seem as unprepossessing as old donkeys pushing a yoke, going in opposite directions but working together.

Nonetheless, in the penultimate stanza of "Lakes," something like the tone of "Mountains" begins to emerge:

> Liking one's Nature, as lake-lovers do, benign
>   Goes with a wish for savage dogs and man-traps:
> One Fall, one dispossession, is enough, I'm sorry;
>   Why should I give Lake Eden to the Nation
> Just because every mortal Jack and Jill has been
>   The genius of some amniotic mere?
>
> [*CSP*, p. 262; *SP*, p. 150]

The paradox of the poem's generally humane view of Nature is that it brings out much in man that is not humane. The last four lines of the stanza present the reasoning of the lake-lover, who, having found his "Lake Eden," deludes himself into thinking that he can return to a prelapsarian innocence and refuses to let anyone else in. Either allowing or refusing entrance to the Nation would destroy the paradisiacal quality, a paradox that suggests that the Edenic quality is illusory.

A passage from Empson's *Some Versions of Pastoral* clarifies (and is a likely source of) the last two lines of the stanza:

> The only passage that I feel sure involves evolution comes at the beginning of *Wonderland* (the most spontaneous and 'subconscious' part of the books) when Alice gets out of the bath of tears that has magically released her from the underground chamber; it is made clear (for instance about watering-places) that the salt water is the sea from which life arose; as a bodily produce it is also the amniotic fluid (there are other forces at work here); ontogeny then repeats phylogeny, and a whole Noah's Ark gets out of the sea with her. In Dodgson's own illustration as well as Tenniel's there is the disturbing head of a monkey and in the text there is an extinct bird. Our minds having thus been forced back onto the history of species there is a reading of history from the period when the Mouse 'came over' with the Conqueror . . .[11]

"Every mortal Jack and Jill" is both a colloquial phrase for "everybody," like "Tom, Dick, and Harry," and a way of saying that everyone who lives and thus will die ("mortal") is a fallen creature (like Jack and Jill, who did indeed fall). Originally, both phylogenically and ontogenically, we all came from water: from the salt water of the sea and from the amniotic fluid of the womb ("mere," in this context, is probably also a translingual pun on mother). It is also worth remembering that Auden is a Lewis Carroll admirer, and that a hint, even indirect, of the Alice books might well serve to exemplify one more comically inverted world in which the physical and psychological status of man is clarified by re-

11. New York: New Directions, 1968, p. 255; 1st publ., 1950.

versal. In any event, the stanza concludes that the believer in
the benignity of nature ignores the truth of man's rise and fall
from nature.

The impulse toward domesticated images of nature, however, is a strong one, with its own truth to it. Tone is crucial,
especially in the last stanza:

> It is unlikely I shall ever keep a swan
>> Or build a tower on any small tombolo,
> But that's not going to stop me wondering what sort
>> Of lake I would decide on if I should.
> Moraine, pot, oxbow, glint, sink, crater, piedmont, dim-
>> ple . . . ?
>> Just reeling off their names is ever so comfy.
>
> [*CSP*, p. 262; *SP.*, p. 150]

John Fuller comments accurately on these lines:

> Critics read this (as they read much of Auden, but this is a no-
> torious example) as unconsciously twee. But surely Auden is
> adjusting, as he continually does, the tone and diction of his medi-
> tation to suit the meaning, and the meaning here is that such Para-
> disal retreats are a dangerous illusion . . . and that contemplation
> of owning one is not only a *comfortable* activity, but, with all
> the social overtones of the phrase, *ever so comfy.*[12]

Dangerous, but psychologically accurate: people prefer to
think of nature sentimentally, as being "ever so comfy"; neither of the views poised against each other, the Darwinian nor
the Christian, allows for this sentimentality, yet the sentimentality must also be taken into account.

"Islands" is a comic rendering of the escape from history
to nature and of the fallacious identification of the lonely, isolated self with "natural man":

12. *Reader's Guide*, p. 220; Fuller's italics.

Obsession with security
In Sovereigns prevails;
His Highness and The People both
Pick islands for their jails.

Once, where detected worldlings now
Do penitential jobs,
Exterminated species played
Who had not read their Hobbes.

[*CSP*, p. 262; *SP*, p. 151]

The logic is comically spurious, and yet it has a point. The reference to Hobbes leads us directly back to arguments concerning civil man and natural man. If those species had read their Hobbes, they might not have "played"; they would have known that they were supposed to be at war. If they had read their Hobbes, they might have learned enough about humans to protect themselves from "extermination," a word that usually refers to the actions of men. Hobbes premised the need for a sovereign on the bestiality of man in a state of nature; that both democratic and monarchical forms of sovereignty perform the inhuman act of returning their enemies—each other—to a Hobbesian state of nature suggests that Hobbes might have been wrong concerning the civility of civil man.

The poem collects, in witty juxtapositions, a congregation of islanders: pirates, deluded saints (whose creaturely nature is perhaps, a kind of millstone), criminals, Napoleons, misanthropes, solipsists. All think they are unique, but the very fact of being susceptible to listing ("Sappho, Tiberius and I") and to conjugation ("They go, she goes, thou goest, I go," which also suggests rote learning) indicates they are wrong. The major comment of the poem comes from its tone, which mocks the assumptions about nature and natural man of both Hobbesian "hard" primitivism and Romantic individualism, describing the islander in terms of pride, aloneness, imprisonment, exile, and solipsism, but suggesting, finally, that these characterize "civil" man as well: "Farmer and fisherman complain / The other has it good." The island character, like the island, is only an inside out turn of the lacustrine.

"Lakes" and "Islands," taken together, present as mirror images an overly humanized, rationalized landscape and the consequent exaltation of the self, both one-sided oversimplifications of man and his relation to nature. Auden makes just this coordination in *The Enchafèd Flood:*

Indeed through the latter half of the seventeenth century and the first half of the eighteenth, there is an attempt in every field, religion, politics, art . . . to found a new Good City on the basis of sound reason, common sense, and good taste.   [*EF,* p. 50]

The Newtonian concept of God as Supreme Architect, he continues, creates a dualism between maker and made, mind and matter. But

Blake and the other romantics along with him tried in their reaction, not to overcome the dualism, but to stand it on its head, i.e., to make God purely immanent, so that to Blake God only acts and is in existing beings and men, or is pantheistically diffused through physical nature, not to be perceived by any exercise of the reason, but only through vision and feeling.

[*EF,* pp. 52–53]

The reflexive dualism described here resembles that existing between "Lakes" and "Islands," and with these poems Auden begins a second cycle of man's history, one that corresponds to the conflict he describes as existing between the Newtonian world view and that of the Romantic reaction. The series is not a precise historical sequence, and I do not mean that Auden is dramatizing specifically the historical conflict between the Enlightenment and Romanticism. Rather, the cycle is in the form of Piero's allegorical representations of man's development; the question is not so much *when* a given phase was reached as the order and nature and interrelationships of the various phases.

"Plains," to follow this hypothesis a step further, completes a second triad of poems by presenting the actualities, both natural and psychological, that both the Newtonian and Romantic views ignore. A plain is the raw stuff that each of the other images is a departure from, and ultimately returns to:

> . . . a mere substance, a clay that meekly takes
> The potter's cuff, a gravel that as concrete
> Will unsex any space which it encloses.
>
> [*CSP*, p. 264; *SP*, p. 152]

Depicted not as landscape but as the absence of landscape, plains have several references that are important to the whole series. Plains are the "neutral passive stuff" of the Newtonian universe, the fundamental material, without embroidery, on which both the Enlightenment and the Romantic reaction to it are based. Plains are closely allied to the image of the desert presented in *The Enchafèd Flood*:

The images of the Just City, of the civilized landscape protected by the Madonna . . . which look at us from so many Italian paintings, and of the rose garden or island of the blessed, are lacking in Romantic literature because the Romantic writers no longer believed in their existence. What exists is the Trivial Unhappy Unjust City, the desert of the average from which the only escape is to the wild, lonely, but still vital sea. The Desert has become, in fact, an image of modern civilization in which innocence and the individual are alike destroyed.   [*EF*, p. 32]

Plains, then, represent the mechanized desert of industrial and postindustrial, technocratic society. They also represent the "abominable desolation" of the self alone in the world: "Which goes to show I've reason to be frightened / Not of plains, of course, but of me" (*CSP*, p. 265; *SP*, p. 154). Like such poems as "The Shield of Achilles" and "Memorial for the City," "Plains" depicts a temporary equation of the historical and natural worlds, imaged by a bleak landscape, identified with, in particular, the modern world, and opposed to sentimental Arcadian wistfulness; at the same time, this is the place of decisive public events, where the strong "chamber with Clio." Fuller suggests that the final phrase, "which is not the case," refers to the world, in the sense that Wittgenstein uses the term "the case," and apparently means, "the way things are." [13] But, ironically, "Plains" approaches very closely both the sense of hard primitivism described by Panofsky in his essay on Poussin and the original Arcadian landscape, which Theocritus forsook for Sicily.

Mythification and demythification work in *Bucolics*, as elsewhere in Auden, like Yeatsian gyres, forever interpenetrating, disappearing into, and creating each other. Having arrived at the desolation represented by plains, the poet moves to "Streams," which celebrates water's "pure being, perfect in music and movement," "the most well-spoken of all the older / servants in the household of Mrs. Nature." The poem is perhaps the purest example of a "verbal rite fittingly done" and, in one sense of the term, the purest "pastoral" in the series. The poem has been praised for itself; it also has an important place in the design of the whole. It has no historical reference; that is part of its point:

13. *Reader's Guide*, pp. 214–215, 221.

             . . . you still
      use the same vocables you were using the day
            before that unexpected row which
       downed every hod on half-finished Babel.
                                    [*CSP*, p. 266; *SP*, p. 155]

Timeless in two senses, the poem portrays a personal vision
of Eden; it is pure pastoral, that is, as Auden has said, a parable
of Grace and Innocence. In "Dingley Dell & The Fleet,"
Auden lists some of the "axioms" of all such dream Edens:

  Eden is a world of pure being and absolute uniqueness. Change
  can occur but as an instantaneous transformation. . . .
  There is no distinction between the objective and subjective. . . .
  Space is both safe and free. There are walled gardens but no
  dungeons, open roads in all directions but no wandering in the
  wilderness.
  Temporal novelty is without anxiety, temporal repetition without boredom. . . .
  Whatever people do, whether alone or in company, is some
  kind of play. . . .
  Three kinds of erotic life are possible, though any particular
  dream of Eden need contain only one. The polymorphous-
  perverse promiscuous sexuality of childhood, courting couples
  whose relation is potential, not actual, and the chastity of natural
  celibates who are without desire. . . .
  The Serpent, acquaintance with whom results in immediate ex-
  pulsion—any serious need or desire.   [*DH*, pp. 410–411]

Later in the same essay he remarks that "No human being is
innocent, but there is a class of innocent human actions called
Games" (*DH*, p. 421). In the end, however, after showing
the Game of Innocence, the writer will "take off the comic
mask and say: 'The Game, the make-believe is over: players

and spectators alike must now return to reality. What you
have heard was but a tall story' " (DH, p. 428). Both the
landscape and the dream at the end of "Streams," and hence
of the whole series, correspond to the prose description of pre-
tend Edens:

> Lately, in that dale of all Yorkshire's the loveliest,
> where, off its fell-side helter-skelter, Kisdon Beck
>   jumps into Swale with a boyish shouting,
>   sprawled out on grass, I dozed for a second,
>
> and found myself following a croquet tournament
> in a calm enclosure, with thrushes popular:
>   of all the players in that cool valley
>   the best with the mallet was my darling.
>
> While, on the wolds that begirdled it, wild old men
> hunted with spades and hammers, monomaniac each,
>   for a megalith or a fossil,
>   and bird-watchers crept through mossy beech-woods.
>
> Suddenly, over the lawn we started to run
> for, lo, through the trees, in a cream and golden coach
>   drawn by two baby locomotives,
>   the god of mortal doting approached us,
>
> flanked by his bodyguard, those hairy armigers in green
> who laugh at thunderstorms and weep at a blue sky:
>   He thanked us for our cheers of homage,
>   and promised X and Y a passion undying.
>
> With a wave of his torch he commanded a dance;
> so round in a ring we flew, my dear on my right,
>   when I awoke. But fortunate seemed that
>   day because of my dream and enlightened,

and dearer, water, than ever your voice, as if
glad—though goodness knows why—to run with the human
    race,
        wishing, I thought, the least of men their
    figures of splendour, their holy places.

[*CSP*, pp. 267–268; *SP*, pp. 156–157]

The play of language and sound complements the images of dream, play, and fancy in a pure Arcadian landscape. Auden, in his record jacket notes, describes the stanza form and rhyme patterns:

In each quatrain, lines 1 and 2 have twelve syllables each and masculine endings, line 3 has nine syllables and a feminine ending. A syllable within line 1 rhymes with a syllable within line 3, the final syllable of line 2 rhymes with the penultimate syllable of line 4, and the penultimate syllable of line 3 rhymes with a syllable within line 4.   [*Caedmon* recording, TC 1019]

John Blair, who was among the first to call attention to the full importance and seriousness of such "verbal playing," characterizes the texture of "Streams" as follows:

The apparently arbitrary imagery and whimsical diction are in part necessitated by the demands of rime and line length, but they serve at the same time to conceal the severity of the demands made on the poet's control over the language. At first encounter the poem appears to be an informal urbane discourse with occasional, almost chance riming and witty puns, like the overtones of "loan" in the "loam" from the "banks" in the [sixth stanza]. Only on close examination does the ingenuity the poet demands from himself become evident.[14]

This seems to me accurate, though perhaps misleading in its suggestion that any one element—diction or imagery—con-

14. *Poetic Art,* p. 150.

ceals the underlying art or is required to make a rhyme. What is most impressive about the poem is the way in which all the verbal and tonal elements participate in its total design and that of the series. The verbal games, the dream, the croquet, the hints of polymorphous-perverse sexuality of childhood, the dream time and dream space, the dancing: all are part of a quixotic figure of Grace. What happens in the dream and what happens in the game is also what happens in the poem; and all these actions are analogues of the vocables of "pure water" and of each other. The requirements of the form, the masculine and feminine endings, the syllable count, and the rhyme of the last syllable in line 2 with the penultimate syllable of line 4, are not very strict; and the other two rhymes allow the poet considerable leeway. Thus, in the first line quoted above, the inversion—"in that dale of all Yorkshire's the loveliest"—is not necessary to get a rhyme; rather, the phrasing creates a certain fastidious formality and sentimental archaism. When the rhymes appear, either in expected or unexpected places, we get the feeling of "temporal novelty without anxiety, temporal repetition without boredom," and the feeling of the movement of water through a creek bed, forever repetitious, and forever novel. When "Kisdon Beck / jumps into Swale with a boyish shouting," the completion of the rhyme with "dale" from the first line figures a movement both free and required, as if Swale, the solid place name, were there to receive the jump. The boyish shouting images the innocent play and prefigures the dream. The consonance and internal rhyming, the mixture of colloquial and archaic diction, the falling dactylic rhythm, as well as the lexical sense of line 2 make a sharp contrast with the smoother and speedier line 3; the jump occurs syntactically and aurally just as the actual jump, across the line break, occurs. The whole poem is constructed with just this exactitude: the interaction of the poem's music with the images, the iconic references, and the "action" is as constant as that among words, phrases, syllables, and sounds.

"Streams" stands in juxtaposition to "Plains," its opposite in almost every sense, but yoked to it by the figure of redemption in "Streams," which is the "answer" to the sterility of the isolated ego in "Plains." The two also represent the sharpest contrast of hard and soft primitivism. "Streams" is the third element of another triadic pattern encompassing the whole series. The first three poems represent in part the movement of man from natural to civil being, both serially and within each poem. The second group, "Lakes," "Islands," and "Plains," represents the movement from civil order to civil sterility and the isolation of the self from both society and nature in a modern desert. The third represents a sense at once renewed and eternal of the benignity of nature and of man's contact, through a return to innocence and a sophisticated playing of games, with nature and with his natural origins; the overall pattern corresponds to the theological patterns of *ante legum, sub lege,* and *sub gratia.*

In each poem a different relation between hard and soft primitivism is portrayed, not so much to debate the merits of either view, or even to say that both have merit but primarily to work toward a definition of man. For Auden, the myth of the historical Fall is, in a sense, a parable of man as simultaneously a creature and a self-aware being, simultaneously a natural, a social, and a spiritual being, simultaneously a part of and separate from nature. The self-qualifying juxtapositions of man, nature, art, and society within the cycle, in continually new combinations, represent and celebrate the multiplicity of man's being. This is the basis of Auden's serious use of the pastoral mode: it allows him to gather together the multiple aspects of man's relation to nature, gives perspective to man's longings to return to a prelapsarian state, celebrates by its artificiality and "unnaturalness" man as a speaking, making, and potentially civil being, mocks his pretensions to be anything else, and draws comic figures of Grace.

No voice in the poem tells us what the relation of the individual poems to each other is. Unlike the two most comparable pieces, *Horae Canonicae* and *Thanksgiving for a Habitat*, there is no occasion or set of events to which we can relate the poems. The poems present themselves as independent, loosely related units that do not specifically comment on each other and that exhibit no overt temporal or narrative form. Even when the underlying structure begins to emerge, we retain the primary sense of seven apparently independent poems arranged in space rather than in time.

This arrangement allows us to look at the individual styles and the individual features of the topography for their own value, even when they refer to a dangerous, foolish, or limited view of the relation of man to nature. It also allows us to separate our evaluations of the several landscapes from our general sense of artistic fullness and topographic variety. This series, like so many of Auden's poems, is full of anachronisms and of suggested correspondences between ontogeny and phylogeny; in its view of time, the Fall is continually reenacted and Paradise continually remembered. We are meant, I believe, to have a sense of the historic as well as the ahistoric character of experience. The poems are exploratory and analytical; almost every view of nature, of man's relation to it, of civility, and of the way art does or does not treat any of these items is present. Hence, the major statement of the poems is the complex conception necessary to a full view of man as a radically multiple being. Finally, as in so much of Auden's art, definition and celebration are carried out simultaneously. The poems, more than anything else, are verbal festivals. Such festivities, one of whose laws of existence is a certain disconnectedness, are in themselves part of the definition of man and the expression of Auden's deepest humanistic impulse.

These hypotheses about the sources, nature, and intention of Auden's pastoral art should raise the question of the use of pastoral in other of his poems. We might ask, for example, whether the laconic haiku poem "Et in Arcadia Ego" (*ATH*, p. 45) is based on Panofsky's essay of that title and where that poem stands in the tradition that Panofsky discusses.[15] It seems to me arguable that the final stanzas of this poem are meant specifically as a rejoinder to Panofsky's kind of humanism:

> I well might think myself
> A humanist,
> Could I manage not to see
>
> How the autobahn
> Thwarts the landscape
> In godless Roman arrogance,
>
> The farmer's children
> Tiptoe past the shed
> Where the gelding knife is kept.   [*ATH*, p. 46]

That is, accepting a progressive view of man as an evolving creature, and even supporting it in some measure by reference to man's progress as a species from "the Brute / Epics and

15. "*Et in Arcadia Ego:* Poussin and the Elegiac Tradition," in *Meaning and the Visual Arts: Papers in and on Art History* (Garden City: Doubleday, 1955), pp. 295–320.

nightmares tell of," the poet still sees both new forms of brutality and old fears. Piero, as presented by Panofsky, had just this ambivalence toward progress beyond a certain point: an evolutionist, he saw the dangers of development to the point of estrangement from nature. The major difference between Auden's humanism and Panofsky's appears to be that Auden argues that "soft" primitivism—the Arcadian spirit in the popular sense—is as necessary to a "realistic" view of man as "hard," evolutionist primitivism; man forever exists in both worlds.

Thus, in "You" (*ATH*, p. 43; *SP*, p. 210), a poem addressed by the ego to the self, the speaker both uses and, in part, quarrels with another source of ideas of *Bucolics:*

> Oh, I know how you came by
> A sinner's cranium,
> How between two glaciers
> The master-chronometer
> Of an innocent primate
> Altered its tempi:
> That explains nothing.
>
> Who tinkered and why?
> Why am I certain,
> Whatever your faults are,
> The fault is mine,
> Why is loneliness not
> A chemical discomfort,
> Nor Being a smell?   [*ATH*, p. 44; *SP*, p. 211]

The first stanza quoted has a clear source in Eiseley's *The Immense Journey:*

The story of Eden is a greater allegory than man has ever guessed. For it was truly man who, walking memoryless through bars of sunlight and shade in the morning of the world, sat down and passed a wondering hand across his heavy forehead. Time and darkness, knowledge of good and evil, have walked with him ever since. It is the destiny struck by the clock in the body in that brief space between the beginning of the first ice and that of the second. In just that interval a new world of terror and loneliness appears to have been created in the soul of man.[16]

The second stanza quoted, which is the last stanza of the poem, says that the purely creaturely definition of man, man thought of solely as a You and not as an I, leaves unanswered crucial questions, questions having to do with being, loneliness, and sin. At the same time, the poem opens with a statement of the insolubility—in both senses of the term—of the bond between ego and self (both the tone and the argument resemble Caliban's speech in *The Sea and the Mirror*, except, of course, that here it is the ego who talks):

> Really, must you,
> Over-familiar
> Dense companion,
> Be there always?
> The bond between us
> Is chimerical surely:
> Yet I cannot break it.   [*ATH*, p. 43; *SP*, p. 210]

Looking at the passage from Eiseley, we readily see that Auden's rejoinder, his insistence that there are facts of man's existence that are unexplained by the evolutionist's parable, is implicit in Eiseley's definition of man: the Fall, in effect, is an evolutionary-biological fact.

Auden is not so much the partisan of one side of a debate as a continual participant in an exploration of man's nature.

16. *The Immense Journey*, p. 125.

f he rejects the kind of humanism that insists on a totally
ecular and rationalist, even materialist, view of man, he is
till a humanist in the root sense. E. M. Forster, referring spe-
ifically to Auden's religious leanings (but admitting that
'Because he once wrote 'We must love one another or die,'
ae can command me to follow him"), writes, "For some of us
vho are non-Christian there still remains the comfort of the
aon-human, the relief, when we look up at the stars, of realis-
ng that they are uninhabitable." [17] Auden responds quite di-
ectly in "The More Loving One":

> Looking up at the stars, I know quite well
> That, for all they care, I can go to hell . . .
>
> If equal affection cannot be,
> Let the more loving one be me.   [*CSP*, p. 282]

This is more by way of good-humored clarification than dispute, as if it say to Forster that he has misunderstood Auden's
eligious feelings, which in fact point toward man, the earth,
and human love rather than toward the heavens and stars.

This reminder returns us to one especially important aspect
of Auden's pastoral. Just as the landscapes in *New Year Let-
er* metaphorically establish man as an earthbound creature,
suited peculiarly to the biosphere, so all of *Bucolics* has the
cumulative effect of placing man and defining his worldli-
ness, telling us, in the words of the epigram to *Bucolics*, with
ts concurrent echoes of Eiseley and Tolkien, that "Fair is
Middle-Earth," and, indeed, celebrating the habitat in which
man finds himself and in which he must act.

Other poems, such as "Ischia" and "In Praise of Lime-

17. "The Game of Life," in *Two Cheers for Democracy* (New
York: Harcourt Brace, 1951), pp. 267, 268.

stone," might also be profitably discussed under the heading
of pastoral; it is clear enough that the pastoral is an important
mode for Auden and that he might well be considered the
major exponent of the pastoral tradition among modern poets
(Frost, for whom the claim is usually made, is perhaps more
appropriately thought of as a georgic—that is, an agricul-
tural—poet than, strictly speaking, a pastoralist.) One important instance, however, remains to be discussed: "The
Shield of Achilles." If I am correct, this poem, widely recognized as one of Auden's masterpieces, is not properly or fully
understood until it is seen in the light of the issues raised by
Bucolics.

A great deal of Auden's art and thought is compressed
into the stately, choric movement and countermovement of
its two stanza forms. As in "On This Island," the interaction
between viewer and view becomes a synecdoche for the relation of man to externality. As in "Musée des Beaux Arts," the
mirror of art serves not only to show the viewer his illusions
but also to define the strengths and limitations of art. As in
The Sea and the Mirror, the relation of maker to audience
becomes a figure for a fundamental human drama that in turn
redefines the relation of artist to the world. As in *For the
Time Being*, the ancient conflict between Christian and classical culture is put into a contemporary idiom that emphasizes
the presence of the past and the pastness of the present. All
these themes meet in "The Shield of Achilles," but more
than anything else, the poem is an elegiac pastoral, in which
Thetis—mother, audience, viewer—represents a principle of
Arcadian sentiment, and Hephaestos—worker, maker, truth-
teller, deformed outcast—represents a principle of honest but
ultimately insufficient realism. The conflict is very much like
that between hard and soft primitivism in *Bucolics*, like that

which, in Panofsky's essay on Poussin, reads "*et in arcadia ego*" to mean "I—death—once dwelt in Arcadia" and that which reads, or misreads, the phrase to mean "I, the shepherd, lived in Arcadia":

> She looked over his shoulder
>   For vines and olive trees,
> Marble well-governed cities
>   And ships upon untamed seas,
> But there on the shining metal
>   His hands had put instead
> An artificial wilderness
>   And a sky like lead.
>
> A plain without a feature, bare and brown,
>   No blade of grass, no sign of neighbourhood,
> Nothing to eat and nowhere to sit down,
>   Yet, congregated on its blankness, stood
>   An unintelligible multitude,
> A million eyes, a million boots in line,
> Without expression, waiting for a sign.
>
> [*CSP*, p. 294; *SP*, p. 135]

Far from showing Thetis the pastoral scene she wishes, Hephaestos, true to his craft, fashions an almost unbearably bleak landscape, at once modern and Greek, in which a ritual crucifixion occurs. Through this scene, and, implicitly, through the crucifixion, the shield finally indicates by negative indirection its own limitation:

> A ragged urchin, aimless and alone,
>   Loitered about that vacancy, a bird
> Flew up to safety from his well-aimed stone:
>   That girls are raped, that two boys knife a third,
>   Were axioms to him, who'd never heard

Of any world where promises were kept,
Or one could weep because another wept.

[*CSP*, p. 295; *SP*, p. 136]

The shield-maker, prototypical artist and also, as Vulcan, prototypical poet and civilizer, cannot show directly the potentiality of redemptive suffering. The poem, however, by combining the soft pastoralism of Thetis and the tough pastoralism of Hephaestos, can indicate both the possibility and the difficulty of salutary sacrifice.

The poise of the poem's oppositions, both among and within stanzas, does not allow for a simple definition of opposing forces as correct and incorrect. Through Hephaestos' handiwork the poem condemns everything in the modern world that robs man of humanity; but Thetis' expectations, her arcadianism, must be seen not simply as wistful sentiment but also as a positive image of possibility; the world of her "soft pastoralism" is a possible world in which promises are kept and in which one can weep.

The poem's dialectic, then, works more subtly and intricately than a simple opposition of illusion and reality. As always in Auden, the mirror of art reflects not only images but also light. Hephaestos' metalworking is appropriate for showing a contemporary world of barbed wire in which mass and measurement predominate and for showing the inevitable end of "Iron-hearted man-slaying Achilles"; its metal reflects perfectly that which is metallic, hence inhuman, in our world: an artificial wilderness and a sky like lead. The poem shows a world in all its bleakness that, nonetheless, can transcend despair. It is perhaps Auden's darkest pastoral (though all pastoral has the potentiality for darkness), his fullest condemnation of a world that denies life. Yet, without in any way dimming its reflection of our world, it suggests, by pro-

jecting the image of Thetis' world of possibility onto Hephaestos' shield, the possibility of that other city of vineyards
and dancing and marriages that the original Homeric armorer
put on the original shield.

5. Acting

Relatively early in his career, Auden suspended consideration of the question of direct action in order to concentrate on the prior questions of man's nature. Increasingly, in the poetry of the fifties and sixties, he has returned to the question without, however, abandoning his insistence that it must be understood in light of the nature of man's existence in the world. The complex forms developed as means of exploring man's nature serve as the means of exploring both the nature of acting and the nature of making, two activities that, to Auden, are closely related.

The question of action is central to *Horae Canonicae*, and can be approached by attempting an Aristotelian definition of the series. The action, we might say, is the movement of a person from the realm of Being into that of Becoming and back again, a vicarious recapitulation of individual growth; the plot is the events of a day. The plot is staged by a governing metaphor that refers to the canonical hours of the church, which in turn are emblematic of the events of Good Friday. This action is presented as a series of poems marking each of the hours.

Or we might say that the action is simply the seven devotions that mark the seven hours. Part of the function of the hours is to signal the devotee to construct his own devotion

hould he be away from the place of common worship, and
his explains the secular tone of the devotions, each of which
:an be viewed as an attempt to relate immediate profane
:xperience to both the liturgical moment and the ritualized
moment of the Passion that it represents; the plot is the human
ittempt to create out of secular materials devotions appropri-
ite to the moment of the liturgy.

Although these hypothetical definitions reveal something,
hey are both somewhat restrictive and suggest a formal strin-
;ency and a linear development that do not in fact exist in
he series. I think there is a more basic action to which the
novements described in my two hypothetical definitions relate
n the manner that diction, plot, character, and spectacle relate
o action in Aristotle's formulation. The action of *Horae
Canonicae*, I propose, is "to act," so that the series is both
n imitation and an exploration of "acting." Auden's explora-
ion of action represents his attempt to fuse and transcend the
notions that we act out of economic, psychological, and bio-
ogical necessity, and the Kierkegaardian notion that we act
ut of the anxiety caused by the freedom that is our condi-
ion. Auden has wanted, I think, to go beyond these definitions
owards a philosophy of significant action and yet to recog-
iize their partial accuracy.

The nature of Auden's concern can be viewed in terms of
. distinction made by Erik Erikson. Erikson, using as starting
ooints Auden's distinction between "behaviour" and "deed"
nd an ambiguity in Freud's use of the term "reality," and
iiming at a notion of action that is attentive to humanistic
bligation, makes a lexical distinction between "reality" and
'actuality."

The term "actuality" will strike us with different connotations
lepending upon whether we are devotees of small or big diction-

aries. The shorter the annotation, the more does "actual" mean the same as "real." "Actuality," thus, can be just another word for phenomenal reality, and yet its linguistic origin vouches for a reality due to a state of being actual, present, current, immediate. It is in the verbs "to activate" and "to actuate" that this meaning has most strongly survived, for what actuates "communicates motion," "inspires with active properties."

I intend here to make the most of this linguistic difference and claim that we must put into their proper relations—sometimes close to identical, sometimes directly antagonistic—that *phenomenal reality* which by psychoanalytic means is to be freed from distortions and delusions, and the meaning of reality as *actuality*—which is participation free (or to be freed) from defensive or offensive "acting out." *Reality* . . . is the world of phenomenal experience, perceived with a minimum of distortion and with a maximum of customary validation . . . while *actuality* is the world of participation, shared with other participants with a minimum of defensive maneuvering and a maximum of mutual activation.[1]

This distinction is at the heart of Erikson's interest in the ability of man not only to adapt to reality but to transform his adaptations into historically and politically significant acts. Without meaning to suggest that Erikson influenced Auden, I think the formulation an interesting focus for a discussion of Auden, who has confronted just those questions that Erikson is dealing with. Specifically, the distinction suggests a view of action based on perceiving and adapting to phenomenal reality but seeking—as Erikson claims Luther and Gandhi sought and found—outlets that transcend the necessities of adaptation and become morally potent. This view

1. "Psychological Reality and Historical Actuality," in *Insight and Responsibility: Lectures on the Ethical Implications of Psychoanalytic Insight* (New York: Norton, 1964), pp. 164–165 (Erikson's italics).

of action moves, as Auden in his perspective poems suggests we must move, beyond the reality principle without denying it. My proposal is that Auden, in *Horae Canonicae*, is presenting an imitation of "action" in the sense of transforming reality into actuality.

This returns us to the formal questions raised by the series, for the action imitated, according to Aristotle, should be "complete, and whole, and of a certain magnitude." A strong case has been made by Robert Adams that the series lacks these qualities. "Prime," he says,

describes the poet's awakening as a quelling of the nocturnal rummage of a rebellious fronde, then as an arrival on earth of Adam sinless, guiltless of any act; and finally as a losing of Paradise. It is hard to see here a developing intention. . . . The total effect is of three unrelated, ingenious metaphors for waking up. The poet is anxious that we be aware that he is aware of the Freudian view of dreams; he disarms us by putting it first. . . .

Thus I think the poet is, throughout the "Horae Canonicae," playing with perspective for its own sake. The Crucifixion story itself is toned down to nothing more than a muted emphasis in a mind largely preoccupied with other things: its guilt, its social comforts, its pleasure in half-significant puns ("holy," "wholly"), off-rhymes, and internal rhymes, its self-consciousness. . . . The poet works so hard to avoid the prophetic and emphatic, he is so versatile in his command of verbal devices and so generous about seeing half-significance for them, that all sense of over-all structure is lost in the murmur and mutter of many muted, restless particulars. The decision to seek this effect was evidently deliberate and is only to be condemned as it makes the poet's own hand (as distinct from his dramatic theme) seem languid, diffuse, and pathetic. There is certainly an over-all shape to the "Horae Canonicae" as a sequence, but it is the arbitrary shape of seven liturgical observations stuffed with a rubble of random thoughts.

With a little cleverness almost anything can be fitted into this form, and the form itself, having nothing to struggle against, takes on the aspect of a sack rather than an architecture.[2]

Adams seems in part to infer likely effect from discernible cause, to assume that there can be no "sense of over-all structure" in a work so busy with particulars and no ultimate seriousness in so self-conscious a work. His commentary raises the questions of how the particulars and how the self-conscious, game-playing artistry compose an overall design, if, indeed, they do. My suggestion is that Auden's large scale constructions are made in much the same way as the smaller patterns. Just as a line of Auden generally involves us in several shifts of diction to create a multiple focus, so the larger works combine several different kinds of discourse into a molecular pattern that defies simple formal description. This mode of organization is a direct result of Auden's attempt to define in a large form the multiplicity of man's experience as a being.

As a starting point toward a definition that would accommodate the various descriptions of the "action" of the sequence suggested above and also the facts of unresolvedness noted by Adams, we might consider Arnold Hauser's characterization of Gothic Art.

The basic form of Gothic art . . . is juxtaposition. Whether the individual work is made up of several comparatively independent parts or is not analyzable into such parts, whether it is a pictorial or a plastic, an epic or a dramatic representation, it is always the principle of expansion and not of concentration, of co-ordination and not of subordination, of the open sequence and not of the closed geometric form, by which it is dominated. The beholder is,

2. *Strains of Discord: Studies in Literary Openness* (Ithaca: Cornell University Press, 1958), pp. 126–127.

as it were, led through the stages and stations of a journey, and the picture of reality which it reveals is like a panoramic survey, not a one-sided, unified representation, dominated by a single point of view. . . . Gothic art leads the onlooker from one detail to another and causes him, as has been well said, to 'unravel' the successive parts of the work one after the other.[3]

This abstract description of form is very similar to that posited in the last chapter for *Bucolics,* and it suggests an architectural relation of parts similar to that existing texturally in the odes and songs; it also resembles the way a work like *The Sea and the Mirror* involves the reader in its workings. It is not quite an exact description of the form of *Horae Canonicae,* mainly because there is a large scale, and extremely important, interplay in the series between the linear movements and the cyclical frame. The notion of form that Hauser describes has the advantage of clearing our minds of the notion that there is—either in this series or in Auden's poetry in general—a hierarchy of elements or movements; it helps focus on the fact that the design of the series is one that juxtaposes a number of elements so that, in a quite literal way, the various materials can be said to mirror and comment on each other. The poem is properly viewed as the movement of a man through a day *and* as an exploration of the nature of man's experience of "being in the world" *and* as a series of devotions *and* as a depiction of both a liturgical ritual and what the rituals emblemize *and* as a presentation of the action of acting. Moreover, form and pattern are not only artistic means but considered subjects in the series. The series is an

3. Arnold Hauser, *The Social History of Art,* trans. Stanley Godman (New York: Knopf, 1952), I, 272–273, as quoted by Charles Muscatine, *Chaucer and the French Tradition: A Study in Style and Meaning* (Berkeley: University of California Press, 1964), pp. 167–168.

arrangement of different kinds of arrangements that excites interest in the various kinds of patterns in which man exists. All of these focuses create a texture of multiple strata, a complex interaction of several different kinds of material, related to Auden's abstract definition of man as a multiple creature.

"Prime" (*CSP*, p. 323; *SP*, p. 157), the first of the poems, is a fine example of the way in which Auden arranges perspectives both to define an experience and to suggest its multiple signification. Its evolution, which can be traced over a period of a decade, demonstrates graphically the way in which Auden uses his art, in the words of Whitehead, "to adjust the language so that it embodies what it indicates" (see *DH*, p. 13) and, indeed, the way in which indication and embodiment interact, each enlarging the scope of the other. We can read "The Dark Years" (*CSP*, p. 176), which was first published in December, 1940, and is about a "brief moment of intersection," both personal and seasonal, as the prototype of "Prime":

> Returning each morning from a timeless world,
> the senses open upon a world of time:
>> after so many years the light is
>> novel still and immensely ambitious,
>
> but, translated from her own informal world,
> the ego is bewildered and does not want
>> a shining novelty this morning,
>> and does not like the noise or the people.
>
> For behind the doors of this ambitious day
> stand shadows with enormous grudges, outside
>> its chartered ocean of perception
>> misshapen coastguards drunk with foreboding.
>
> [*CSP*, p. 176]

Much of the thematic material of "Prime" is present in "The Dark Years": not only the focus on the moment of awakening, but also the attempt to show the moment as a balance between parts of the self, the projection of this balance onto larger screens—in this case, the seasonal moment and a point in history—and the use of syntax and stanzaic arrangement to create the sense of the moment and of the coordinates of which it is the intersection. The mode is still primarily descriptive: Auden seems still to be exploring the problem of achieving a feeling of stopped time while the reader's direct verbal experience, the linear movement of the structure, is of temporal movement; the poem moves forward, and the sense of suspended transitoriness that marks the final version is missing.

In a lecture given in 1950,[4] Auden takes what for him is the unusual step of discussing in detail the genesis and making of a poem of his own. As an illustration of the points made in what finally appears as "The Virgin & The Dynamo" in *The Dyer's Hand*, Auden discusses the metamorphosis of the final version of "Prime" from an original draft (he does not mention "The Dark Years"), copies of which he distributed to the audience. His general theme is that poetry is an attempt to transform a crowd of memories into a verbal community, using the terms "crowd" and "community" with precision and placing great weight on their meanings. The original version of the poem, as duplicated for the lecture, opens as follows:

4. 9 March 1950, at Swarthmore College; see Spears, *Auden,* pp. 317–318 and 345n. I am grateful to Mr. Howard Williams, Reference Librarian of the Swarthmore College Library, for supplying me with a tape of the lecture and for unearthing a copy of the poem that Auden distributed to the audience, and to Mr. Auden for permission to quote from the poem.

> Simultaneously as at the instant
> Word of the light the gates of the body,
> The eyes and the ears open
> Into its world beyond,
> The gates of the mind, the horn gate, the ivory gate,
> Swing to, shut off
> The nocturnal rummage of its angry fronde,
> Crippled and second-rate,
> Still suffering from some historical mistake.

There are a number of differences between this and the comparable passage from "The Dark Years," but the pattern is still progressive and linear, and, indeed, the Horatian stanza form of the earlier poem accomplishes some of the things that the final form of "Prime" does. The description is of the momentariness of the movement from the timeless world to the world of time, but the movement is itself fully in time, and the reverberations are additive, so that the "brief moment of intersection" is, verbally, in motion.

The point is best appreciated by looking at the final version of "Prime":

> Simultaneously, as soundlessly,
>   Spontaneously, suddenly
> As, at the vaunt of the dawn, the kind
>   Gates of the body fly open
> To its world beyond, the gates of the mind,
>   The horn gate and the ivory gate
> Swing to, swing shut, instantaneously
>   Quell the nocturnal rummage
> Of its rebellious fronde, ill-favoured,
>   Ill-natured and second-rate,
> Disenfranchised, widowed and orphaned
>   By an historical mistake:
> Recalled from the shades to be a seeing being,

From absence to be on display,
    Without a name or history I wake
        Between my body and the day.

[*CSP*, p. 323; *SP*, p. 157]

Auden chose his example of a crowd being transformed into a verbal community perfectly; "Prime" is an instance not of a form being found to accommodate an idea but of a complex group of ideas creating an appropriate form. The four almost rhyming polysyllabic adverbs of the first two lines are suspended, since the verbs they modify are withheld; quality is suspended from action. The series of similar words "freezes" the qualities, while their fluid tone and the fact that all are adverbs maintains an effect of transience and elusiveness. Although the four words seem to be a series, "simultaneously" modifies "swing to, swing shut" in line seven, whereas the three succeeding words modify "fly open" in line four. Appropriately, "simultaneously" links three pairs of actions: the movement of the gates of the body with that of the gates of the mind; the movement of the horn gates (true dreams) with that of the ivory gates (false dreams); and these actions with the break of dawn: the movement of words imitates the "actual" movement. This linkage creates the illusion that all these things happen in an instant; the verbal pattern creates a "now," a gap of time.

We can paraphrase the first seven lines of "Prime" as follows: when, at the break of dawn, the body awakens, then, at the same instant, the dual gates of the mind open and close. But much more happens in these lines. (In his lecture on the poem's composition Auden tells of the time and care that he spent finding the words and patterns to embody precisely the sensations that are his subject.) The subject of the sentence ("gates of the mind") is withheld until the fifth line, poised against the counterimage ("gates of the body") in the fourth line and expanded by the appositional sixth line ("the horn gate and the ivory gate"), which also suspends the parallel verb of the seventh line: "swing to, swing shut." This action occupies the center of the stanza and of the sentence; the balance of internal and external actions and the movement of simultaneous opening and closing recurs in each line. The whole stanza creates a diagram of this moment, a moment at once unique and paradigmatic. The construction forces us to the center of the stanza, where a complex subject (gates, modified by "gate" and "gate," and poised against still another gate) governs a complex verb ("swing to, swing shut"); and as we work both backward and forward the balancing continues along several coordinates, with internal rhyming underscoring the balances of images and syntax. The vaunt of the dawn, a striking image in itself, precedes the nocturnal rebellion, which it succeeds temporally, suspending the moment and at the same time asserting the triumph of the external world over the internal self. The world of dreams, described in "The Dark Years" as the ego's "own informal world," is introduced in "Prime" by the rhetorical device of congeries. The list of adjectives of derogation—"ill-favored, ill-natured, and second-rate"—is purposely overstated, and the effect is magnified by the parallel series that functions both as adjectives and passive verbs—"disenfranchised, widowed and orphaned." The "historical mistake" by which the fronde has been disenfranchised has a multiple meaning: man has fallen into history and into time, by the historical, in the sense of epochal, mistake: the self as a purely natural being is disenfranchised by the mistake of evolution, and the moment of waking disenfranchises the rebellious natural, private self. The political and civil terminology (fronde, rebellion, widow, orphan) makes its point by reversal: man emerges into the civil world from the natural by these acts of disenfranchisement.

The last lines of the stanza recapitulate the moment, and, at the same time, introduce a new diagram for the moment. It is important that "I" is used here for the first time, because, at the moment of "betweenness," the "I" does not exist: only the abstracted body, mind, and world. But, paradoxically, by moving forward in time, by dissolving the stasis wrought in the preceding lines, the "I" emerges in time. Each of the four lines is a balance, further emphasized by the internal rhyming and the repetition of words: "to be a seeing being," moving from infinitive to gerund, hence from potentiality to duration and actuality, summarizes the movement the whole stanza diagrams. As dramatized by the syntax, the stanza recounts in minute detail and slow motion the emergence of the "I," the entire person.

The second stanza of "Prime" praises that instant in which the "I" emerges from the "nocturnal rebellion," in which it recognizes the world around it but is not yet involved in that world:

> Holy this moment, wholly in the right,
>   As, in complete obedience
> To the light's laconic outcry, next
>   As a sheet, near as a wall,
> Out there as a mountain's poise of stone,
>   The world is present, about,
> And I know that I am, here, not alone
>   But with a world and rejoice
> Unvexed, for the will has still to claim
>   This adjacent arm as my own,
> The memory to name me, resume

> Its routine of praise and blame,
> And smiling to me is this instant while
>   Still the day is intact, and I
> The Adam sinless in our beginning,
>   Adam still previous to any act.
>
> [*CSP*, p. 323; *SP*, pp. 157–158]

The phrasing, though still intricate, and still effecting a suspension of the instant, becomes less involved, less periodic,
with four coordinate clauses that explain the verbless assertion
of the first line. Whereas the first stanza looks back from the
emergence of the "I" in the seventeenth line to the nocturnal
rebellion and is mixed in vocabulary, complex in metaphor,
and intricate in construction, the second stanza dwells on the
moment in its wholeness, its "betweenness," and its detachment from the world and the body, the night and the day. It is
simple, almost childish in diction, figure, and phrasing. The
punning on "holy" is important not simply as an assertion
of the relation between wholeness and a kind of holiness, but
also, in its simplicity, as an indication of the state of mind
being dramatized. The figures of speech—next as a sheet,
near as a wall, out there as a mountain's poise of stone—are
brilliant in their simplicity and their accuracy, and they work
with the other elements to create an atmosphere of fresh discovery, of seeing for the first time and trying to put experiences into words, and of arriving at the proximate, but deftly
precise word. By the time the overt comparison to prelapsarian being is made, the ambience of a naive paradise has been
created by the words, and the speaker has established himself
with a kind of open-eyed innocence. The devices are artfully
simple, but the artificiality is part of the intended effect, for
the speaker is an artificial and momentary Adam, about to
fall abruptly.

At the end of the second stanza of "Prime," then, the speaker is "still previous to any act" and thus sinless. Unlike the first two stanzas, the third begins with a simple assertion of an action:

> I draw breath; that is of course to wish
>   No matter what, to be wise,
> To be different, to die and the cost,
>   No matter how, is Paradise
> Lost of course and myself owing a death . . .
>   [*CSP*, p. 324; *SP*, p. 158]

The transience of the quasi-paradise is made clear by the immediacy with which action follows the passive Adamic state of stanza two and by the intentionally bad play on "Paradise / Lost," with "lost" momentarily delayed by the line break but made all the more emphatic by the delayed rhyme with "cost." The incompleteness described in the second stanza as the source of the paradisiacal state is now completed, though the completion is in another sense the loss of completeness: the "I" has claimed its body, has a name and a history and a "share of care." Here the sentence structure creates the effect of continuous action, as opposed to that of suspension in the first two stanzas. Conspicuous is the self-perpetuating structure in which a word completes a phrase and at the same time begins a new phrase; thus, in the instance cited, "Paradise" completes the predication of "cost" and also extends it into the next line; as one pattern is completed, a new one grows out of the completing agent. This is, in part, simply a change from complex syntax to compound, additive structures, but the change is more complicated. The basic rhetorical pattern is the diazeugma, the governance of more than one verb by a single subject, a pattern of some intricacy here, since verbs are governing other verbs. Hence, "to draw breath" is "to wish to be wise," but it is not immediately clear if the next infinitives, "to be different" and "to die," are governed by "to wish" or parallel to it. On the basis of sense, it seems more likely that the poem says that drawing breath, as the beginning of life, is also the origin of difference and death. The effect is intricate continuity; just as word patterns work in the first stanza to stop motion, to make everything turn on a single instant, here they work to make every moment produce a new moment, every action lead to another:

> The eager ridge, the steady sea,
> The flat roofs of the fishing village
>   Still asleep in its bunny,
> Though as fresh and sunny still are not friends
>   But things to hand, this ready flesh
> No honest equal, but my accomplice now,
>   My assassin to be, and my name
> Stands for my historical share of care
>   For a lying self-made city,
> Afraid of our living task, the dying
>   Which the coming day will ask.

> [CSP, p. 324; SP, p. 158]

The additive phrasing keeps bringing eventual outcome into coordination with initial cause, indicating that existence in the historical world of time is always progressive; hence the poetry always leads us to the end—the assassination or the death—before we expect it. Nonetheless, there is still a stasis here, between potentiality and completion, summed up, perhaps, by the phrase "to hand." In his lecture Auden said that the phrase came from his reading of Heidegger. It means roughly the same thing in Heidegger's writings as it does in common usage; discussing it in some detail, however, may help to reveal the series' essential subject.

"The kind of Being which equipment possesses," Heidegger says, "we call *'readiness-to-hand.'* "[5] Being, to Heidegger, is the primordial mode of existing that things have, and is the mode that philosophy properly should aim to discover. In this instance, Heidegger suggests that we try to approach Being by understanding the way in which our world conceived as a world of equipment, of utensils, exists for us. Entities in this world are entangled in their intended use, the materials of which they are made, and the things we might use them for. But they also have a more fundamental aspect, "presence-at-hand," which can be discovered by carefully disregarding the usefulness of the utensils.

Hence, "when something ready-to-hand is found missing, though its everyday presence . . . had been so obvious that we have never taken any notice of it, this makes a *break* in those referential contexts which circumspection discovers," that is, in the ties it has to the practical world. When this break occurs, "the environment announces itself afresh" (p. 105). We have glimpsed Being. "To hand," then, refers in the poem to a quality either of utility or of a pointed lack of utility that has the potential of laying bare Being in a primary mode.

In the poem we move from Being towards utility, from simple presence to complex readiness. The ridge is doubly eager: it has, at the moment of waking, the quality of authentic Being disclosing itself; but it, like the other items in the world, is about to become equipment; it seems eager to be used, and hence is about to lose its primal freshness.

Here a new sense of "prime" emerges. Besides being the first canonical hour and the moment of waking, it is also that which is philosophically primary, that is, Being. And, as the poem moves from stasis into time, that primordial entity is

5. *Being and Time*, p. 98; Heidegger's italics.

about to lose its unitary quality; the loss of Paradise is meant to stand for our loss of direct apprehension of Being. This use of the Fall as metaphor may also have been suggested by Heidegger, who says that "Being-in-the-world is always fallen" (p. 225).

Another line in the third stanza of "Prime," "historical share of care," may have the same origin. For Heidegger, "care" is a crucial word, ultimately connected with the historical character of Being and with the emergence of selfhood. Like "to hand," "care" is difficult to describe without using a terminology at least equally elusive. "Care" is an essential aspect of Being and of temporality: *"Temporality reveals itself as the meaning of authentic care,"* and "Care is Being-towards-death." [6] For Heidegger, there is a kind of hierarchy consisting of fear, dread, and care. Fear is always of something; dread is general fear without an object; and care is a kind of transmutation of dread into a more positive state of taking care of, being concerned with, and being anxious about. We "care" about the world into which we, in effect, fall. "Care," then, is the highest response to authentic being. Hence, a "historical share of care" is an acknowledgment of a certain responsibility that is connected to the temporality of the world. Just as the Creation and the Fall are used as metaphors for aspects of existence, so also is the Crucifixion, which dominates the series, as an emblem of the connection between Being and Death.

"Prime" creates the illusion that we are directly experiencing waking; its images of the "out thereness" of the world— "next / As a sheet, near as a wall, / Out there as a mountain's poise of stone"; "The eager ridge, the steady sea"—are completely compelling. At the same time, consciousness is con-

6. *Being and Time*, pp. 374, 378; Heidegger's italics.

tinually enlarging, as the speaker begins to explain, digest, and mythify the experience. These movements are both diagrammatic and mimetic of the whole experience: by the balancing of perspectives we are given the sense of multiplicity and diffusion that, save for a brief moment of paradisiacal intactness, are the qualities of our experience. Adams objects to the self-consciousness and "half-significant puns" of the poem, but seems to me to miss the developmental quality: "Prime" is marked by a growing self-consciousness that is a part of the poem's attempt to represent and define experience with exactitude. The poem can be seen as a small rite of homage to that instant in which Paradise and the primariness of experience—its briefly undivided quality—are glimpsed, and which thus allows the actor to begin his daily tasks with knowledge of exactly where he is.

The text of the poem is, in effect, the first chapters of Genesis: the Creation, Adam in Paradise, and the Fall. But this larger reference is itself emergent: even as the poem moves through the three moments of waking, the significance of the three stages enlarges. These stages are in turn part of a larger structure created by the first three poems in the series, which, in a broader circle of reference, again bring the Creation, the Fall, and the Crucifixion together. After the richness of "Prime," the next two poems, especially "Terce," seem slight, but the pattern of the three poems taken together makes a larger structure of intricacy and substance.

"Terce" (CSP, p. 324; SP, p. 159) deals with an easily overlooked instant, one which "the Big Ones / Who can annihilate a city / Cannot be bothered with": that instant before the machinery of the world and of action—and hence, metaphorically, the machinery of the Crucifixion—is set in motion. After the intensity of "Prime," "Terce" is relaxed and detached in manner, its point of view panoramic and ironic. Its structure is triadic, on both the largest and smallest scales. The first stanza presents sketches of three apparently unrelated scenes, each sketch economical in its choice of slight gestures that imply a full and yet more or less stereotyped drama. It implies by its parallels that the actions described are analogous and perhaps interrelated: three homely jobs are to be done, three abstractions to be satisfied. The sketches define the sphere of action that exists between the insignificant, private acts like shaking paws with a dog, caring for a wife with a headache, and taking a stroll in a garden and abstract ideals like Justice, Law, and Truth. In each case the agent's private gesture has little to do with the public act. By comparing the hangman and the judge, both of whom will in fact kill during the day, with the poet, who will only write a poem, Auden continues the suggestion of "Prime" that the Crucifixion is a symbol for any and all acts, the prototypical end of acting itself, just as the Fall is a symbol for all awakenings. The phrasing and the arrangement of "Terce" are deceptively simple: they create a double focus on agent and act by a series of inversions. There is the larger inversion of execution, law, and truth, emphasized by the anaphoras that spell out point by point comparisons, with each phrase beginning "he does not know," and the small scale inversions of phrasing, as, for example, in "He does not know yet who will be provided / To do the high works of Justice with." Each agent moves toward an act that is both inevitable and unknown, and every element of the poem dramatizes the combination of certainty and uncertainty of the moment, making the reader look simultaneously at the completed object and the movement toward it, as if one saw a man leaving a railway station and arriving at his destination simultaneously.

The pattern is diagrammed in the third stanza, which itself moves from "this hour" to "good Friday":

> At this hour we all might be anyone:
>   It is only our victim who is without a wish
>   Who knows already (that is what
>   We can never forgive. If he knows the answers,
>   Then why are we here, why is there even dust?),
>   Knows already that, in fact, our prayers are heard,
>   That not one of us will slip up,
>   That the machinery of our world will function
>   Without a hitch, that today, for once,
>   There will be no squabbling on Mount Olympus,
>   No Chthonian mutters of unrest,
>   But no other miracle, knows that by sundown
>   We shall have had a good Friday.
>
> [CSP, p. 325; SP, pp. 159–160]

The parenthesis underscores the double focus. Man is placed between the completed, known act and the potential to act: in the first stanza of "Terce" there is a choric "does not know"; in the third, this becomes "knows already." At this moment, man is briefly trivial, and prays to an image of an image of himself. Since nothing has yet been done, man is silly, trite, incomplete, even if in a fetching way; since what will be done will be a form of crucifying, his prayer "to get through this coming day" is portentous.

"Sext" (CSP, p. 325; SP, p. 160) celebrates those very activities that are the basis at once of civilization (the escape from pure natural law) and of Sin and Death (the accompanying result of man's escape from nature). Each of the first two parts celebrates what is referred to in "Terce" as "the machinery of our world," what Heidegger calls "equipment"; the third section contrasts these specific acts of civilization with today's civilization. The latter is described as "the crowd," a group "whose only relation is arithmetical" (*DH*, p. 63). From this description the poem moves dialectically toward the conclusion that only because "the crowd rejects no one," "can we say / all men are our brothers." Men, when reduced to the lowest common denominator of anonymity as members of the crowd, still have a potentiality for transformation into a higher order of plurality; the unfreedom and the disorder of the historical world of fallen man can be redeemed into actuality; "the unfreedom and disorder of the past can be reconciled in the future" (*DH*, p. 70). Auden contrasts man with "the social exoskeletons," the insects who are at least man's equal in social organization and energy but, being solid brained, incapable of consciousness, are unfallen and hence unredeemable. Man must fall from nature even to have the potential to achieve the order of "community," a group united "by a common love of something other than themselves" (*DH*, p. 64), because such love depends on consciousness.

The first two parts of "Sext" focus on a series of acts in which the agents are seen "forgetting themselves in a function," the third on the total disappearance of self in the crowd. This completes a movement, begun in "Prime" and carried on in "Terce," by which the human self slowly emerges from his natural existence, establishes relations with the world, moves into the sphere in which other people exist, and achieves a kind of anonymity that resembles, but is not quite identical with, the anonymity of the natural world: the journey into the historical world has been taken, and can only be forgotten or ignored, not denied. The journey is an allegory of the modern age, explained abstractly in "The Virgin & The Dynamo" (the essay that grew out of Auden's lecture on "Prime"). Using the terms of that essay, we may describe the journey as from the "real" natural world into the "real" historical world of potentiality into the "chimerical" world of history, "the mechanized history created by the scientific illusion which would regard the world of faces as if it were a world of masses" (DH, p. 62). In the first three poems, then, we move into a world of potential civility and community and from there into a modern, mechanized desert of human anonymity.

There are parallel movements in manner and in perspective: from the personal to the detached, and from the introspective and subjective through the focused objective to the panoramic. The "I" that emerged in "Prime" and was seen on the brink of acting in "Terce" is lost in the abstract third person description of "Sext." "Sext" has none of the surface busyness of "Prime," little of the syntactical complication. Spears describes it as "deliberately prosaic," [7] but this is not quite accurate; "prosaic" suggests the kind of homeliness of "Terce" but not the almost classical sparseness and stringency of vocabulary and phrasing in "Sext":

> You need not see what someone is doing
> to know if it is his vocation,
>
> you have only to watch his eyes:
> a cook mixing a sauce, a surgeon
>
> making a primary incision,
> a clerk completing a bill of lading,
>
> wear the same rapt expression,
> forgetting themselves in a function.

7. *Auden,* p. 319.

How beautiful it is,
that eye-on-the-object look.

[*CSP*, pp. 325–326; *SP*, p. 160]

The style is conspicuously bare, but at the same time almost fastidiously careful, using constructions that make no jumps and leave out no steps whatsoever; its rhetoric is governed by "hypozeuxis" ("every clause in a sentence has its own subject and verb" [8]). The poem is neither verbose nor terse, but, rather, exact, and the diction is simple, latinate, and somewhat technical. The painstaking manner of "Sext" is the precise equivalent of the impersonal concentration on a job being done; the poem embodies that "eye-on-the-object look."

Upon this framework of simplicity two lines of irony are quietly developed. The first comes from the unexpected linking of various makers of civilization: the surgeon with the cook and the clerk, the general with the bacteriologist and the prosecuting attorney. These linkings show civilization not as the embodiment of civility but as an unordered collection of small triumphs of creation. The second line of irony is the result of the mocking refrain at the end of each part:

and, at this noon, for this death,
there would be no agents.   [*CSP*, p. 326; *SP*, p. 161]

and, at this noon, there would be no authority
to command this death.   [*CSP*, p. 328; *SP*, p. 162]

at this noon, on this hill,
in the occasion of this dying?   [*CSP*, p. 329; *SP*, p. 164]

Each of the series of acts leads to this death: that it does is not a rejection but a definition of action.

8. Lanham, *Handlist*, p. 58.

The pattern of "Sext" is more complicated than it looks. First, the deeds described become increasingly ominous, moving from those of the lonely "makers" of the first section, to the commanders of the second, to the crowd, with its complete destruction of individual identity, in the third; these are both parallel and serial movements. At the same time, the crowd of the third section is the unlikely instrument of potential redemption of itself:

> Few people accept each other and most
> will never do anything properly,
>
> but the crowd rejects no one, joining the crowd
> is the only thing all men can do.
>
> Only because of that can we say
> all men are our brothers.   [*CSP*, p. 329; *SP*, p. 164]

This paradox is crucial to the whole series and, in fact, is Auden's version of the fortunate Fall and fortunate Crucifixion. Fortunately fallen from nature into history, man as a free agent commits inevitable crimes against his own flesh by misusing, or trying to escape from, his freedom. "Sext," which moves from innocent making to "surrender of freedom," describes the almost inevitable loss of a sense of intactness that occurs when man acts. His loss is ultimately good because it prepares him for an acceptance of his fallen state that is the necessary condition for acts that are "deeds" rather than "behaviour" and thus can redeem time.

Each successive poem adds to the thick texture of the series. Part of this quality results from the interweaving of abstract statement, devotional ritual, dramatized experience, and the biblical stories of the Fall and the Crucifixion: even to classify the strata in this manner is to risk reducing the texture to a scheme. This kind of texture opens the series to the charge of incompleteness and "half-significance," but it also reveals the way in which Auden regards the complex relation between religious myth and actual experience. Fundamentally, the series assumes that religious myths are parables of man's experience, that the Fall, for example, is a parable of man's experience of being "thrown into" the world and the Crucifixion a parable of man's sense of action as simultaneously loss and a possible means of redemption. Thus stated, Auden sounds close to the heresy of reducing doctrine to drama, but this is not the case. Auden works from a notion of Christian myth as an extraordinarily accurate parable of experience, and the series seeks to exploit the rich relations between the two.

The balance is most thoroughly maintained in "Nones" (*CSP*, p. 330; *SP*, p. 164). The poem is the copestone of the series and, in some ways, the most difficult poem to characterize. It lacks the ostentation of rhetorical and poetic devices that characterizes the first three poems, but it weaves threads from all three into the richest poetic texture of the series. Thematically, it is a mirror image of the first three poems, because it moves from the world of pure act back to the world of not quite pure being: not quite, because the act having been committed, the paradisiacal state cannot be wholly regained.

The hour of "Nones" covers the period described in Matthew, Mark, and Luke at which, between the sixth and ninth hours, following the Crucifixion, a great darkness blotted out all light; it is also the sleepy siesta hour of the Mediterranean town suggested at several points in the series. The poem is in one sense audaciously vague, talking about "the deed," "our feat," "this event," without specifying what act s being discussed. At the same time, it is specific in its use of concrete images,[9] those brilliant "glimpses of life" that Bayley finds to be characteristic of Auden's best poetry:

The situations that appear and recur . . . with such vividness are of the kind which we can imagine occurring to the poet as he closes his eyes for a liberating instant between two minutes of actual living. They are glimpses of life, brilliantly concrete, but seen from the unparticipating outside, as we see the screen when sitting in the cinema.[10]

They seem, he continues, to "take place 'altogether elsewhere' "; they exist "startlingly clear of their contexts." In "Nones" there are suggestions of scenes and of various actions, but most of the imagery is generalized, and refers to no specific landscape:

> The spell of the asparagus garden,
>   The aim of our chalk-pit game; stamps,
> Birds' eggs are not the same, behind the wonder
>   Of tow-paths and sunken lanes . . .
>   wherever
> The sun shines, brooks run, books are written,
>   There will also be this death.   [*CSP*, p. 331; *SP*, p. 166]

To follow Bayley's apt film analogy, this stanza consists of statements illustrated by a series of stills, each of them powerful and most of them stereotyped images that imply psy-

9. A good example is the reference to the three Madonnas. "At the University of Massachusetts on March 15, 1967, Auden said that these three Madonnas could not be found anywhere outside of the poem" Susan Jeanne Moore [Johnson], "W. H. Auden: The Emergence of Distinctive Voice," thesis, Mount Holyoke College, 1967, p. 86, n21). From this work I received the suggestion of "The Dark Years" as a prototype for "Prime" (see pp. 12–13).

10. *Romantic Survival*, p. 137.

chological significance without stating it. They are held together by a mood of ominousness and by the internal rhyming, but they lack pictorial continuity; they resemble the dream landscape used in the penultimate stanza. The discrepancy between the weight of the imagery and the vagueness of the event is explainable, first, by the notion of the Crucifixion as emblematic of all actions, and second, by a view of the relation between guilt and sin. The act, the sin, itself buried and almost unimportant, has consequences and repercussions, both physical and psychological, that are present, vivid, insistent, and are related to each other and to the act itself according to laws of association. By using a dreamscape collage of psychologically potent but logically unconnected images, Auden renders the hours of darkness following the deed.

As a backdrop to this picture "Nones" develops the images of the sleepy town and, in the last stanza, of "our own wronged flesh," "restoring / The order we try to destroy, the rhythm / We spoil out of spite" (*CSP*, p. 332; *SP*, p. 167). A cycle is completed. "Nones" returns us to the point from which "Prime" embarked, with the body a purely natural organism, the mind in a rebellion of dreams, and the "I" nonexistent.

The degree to which "Nones" lacks the chartable form of the first three poems but still remains an ordered poem is of some importance. Degree and kind of order are means and theme in the series. The poem refers to and embodies several kinds of order, thus again defining man as a multiple being. At one extreme are

> The faceless many who always
> Collect when any world is to be wrecked,
> Blown up, burnt down, cracked open,

Felled, sawn in two, hacked through, torn apart.

[*CSP*, p. 330; *SP*, p. 165]

The congeries, with epithet piled on top of epithet, is a rhetorical trope for the sheer arithmetical and random plurality of the crowd. At the other extreme is the order of nature,

> . . . the rhythm
> We spoil out of spite: valves close
> And open exactly, glands secrete,
> Vessels contract and expand
> At the right moment, essential fluids
> Flow to renew exhausted cells,
> Not knowing quite what has happened, but awed
> By death.   [*CSP*, p. 332; *SP*, p. 167]

The Public is a modern, *the* modern instance of a crowd, at once the least significantly organized kind of plurality and the most orderly, in the sense that, each of its members being faceless, none is unique. The order of nature is a society: "in the natural world of the Dynamo, communities do not exist, only societies which are submembers of the total system of nature, enjoying their self-occurrence" (*DH*, p. 64). People and poems—life and art—both strive for the third kind of order, that of community.

According to the Gospels Christ was crucified at the third hour, terce, nine in the morning. At sext, the sixth hour, noon, the great darkness fell over the earth, lasting until nones, the ninth hour, three in the afternoon, when "He took to the ghost, and the veil of the temple was rent." The rending of the veil, which separates the sacrosanct area of the Holy of Holies in the temple from the multitude, signifies that Christ's sacrifice removes barriers between God and man and completes the original intention of the Incarnation.

Nones is, then, the dénouement of the drama of the Passion. It is also an instance of the ambivalence of the Crucifixion: something bad in itself that produces good results. Like the rending of the veil, it breaks down an old order that a new and better order may emerge, specifically one in which the distinction between the area of sacredness and that of profanity no longer exists. In part, it represents the movement of divinity from a spatial onto a temporal plane. God is no longer in a place; He is a part of history.

Just this ambivalence about the Crucifixion exists in "Nones," and in the whole sequence. At the end of "Sext," a chimerical order corresponding to the "crowd" exists, a regression in terms of the preceding sections of the poem and of the series. The act is then committed and has the positive effects of dissolving the malevolent plurality that commits it and of making possible the formation of a community; the "we" that emerges in "Nones" hints at this possibility.

I think "Nones" is in part an attempt to dramatize the "crowd of historical events" that the artist seeks "to transform into a verbal community" and that its relatively loose, additive, inclusive form serves as an emblem of the Crucifixion. Its kind of order, built around the voice of the speaker rather than on a simple triadic structure, contrasts with the progressively constricting order of the first three poems. The effect is to have at the center of the series a picture of man existing in historical time between natural rhythmical order and chimerical historical order, between Crucifixion and redemption, between myth and experience, forever divorced from original innocence and yet in need of some sort of belief in it.

The next poem, "Vespers" (CSP, p. 333; SP, p. 168), marks the hour of communal worship and presents still another kind of verbal order, that of prose. The appropriateness of the prose is immediately apparent: "Vespers" pictures man as a prosaic being, heading in two directions, by using two possible images of "the Happy Place" where "good and evil are unknown." The matter of perspective in "Vespers" is not so simple as it appears. The speaker identifies himself as the Arcadian and his "anti-type" as a Utopian but proceeds by counterpointing each of the beliefs of each type to suggest not only balance but complementarity:

Was it (as it must look to any god of cross-roads) simply a fortuitous intersection of life-paths, loyal to different fibs?

Or also a rendezvous between two accomplices who, in spite of themselves, cannot resist meeting

to remind the other (do both, at bottom, desire truth?) of that half of their secret which he would most like to forget,

forcing us both, for a fraction of a second, to remember our victim (but for him I could forget the blood, but for me he could forget the innocence),

on whose immolation (call him Abel, Remus, whom you will, it is one Sin Offering) arcadias, utopias, our dear old bag of a democracy are alike founded:

For without a cement of blood (it must be human, it must be innocent) no secular wall will safely stand.

[*CSP*, p. 335; *SP*, p. 170]

At first the poem presents utopianism and arcadianism as harmless escapes; it shows the two impulses as poles between which we exist in time, as the unachieved but possible community that we may at some point create and the once actual but now vanished paradise of natural being from which we have fallen. Of the one we have glimpses in the achieved perfection of art, of the other we have mnemonic traces at the moment of waking. If we confuse either with actuality, we are in danger of creating chimerical worlds; and if we act on the basis of chimeras rather than realities, we are in danger of acting wrongly and destructively. Perceived not as possible future and instructive atavism but as immediately realizable actualities, both blur the fact of man's existence in time, which is described well by the parable of the Crucifixion. The balancing of the two impulses against each other presents both poles of experience as equally dangerous escapes. The last paragraph states both Auden's commitment to the building of "secular walls" and his conviction that their building must be based on a view of man as he is. These lines are what mark the fortune of the Crucifixion, for if the secular wall must be cemented with human, innocent blood, the "events" of the first four poems that lead to the "act" in "Nones" also are preparation for building the wall; that it is in prose rather than verse suggests a kind of ethical seriousness about the wall that must be built.[11]

11. In *A Certain World: A Commonplace Book* (London: Faber and Faber, 1971), Auden comments at some length on Good Friday and on his relation to the events: "Christmas and Easter can be subjects for poetry, but Good Friday, like Auschwitz, cannot. . . . Just as we were all, potentially, in Adam when he fell, so we were all, potentially, in Jerusalem on that first Good Friday before there was an Easter, a Pentecost, a Christian, or a Church. It seems to me worth while asking ourselves who we should have been and what we should have been doing. None of us, I'm certain, will imagine himself as one of the Disciples, cowering in agony of spiritual despair and physical terror. Very few of us are big wheels enough to see ourselves as Pilate, or good churchmen enough to see ourselves as a member of the Sanhedrin. In my most optimistic mood I see myself as a Hellenized Jew

"Compline" (*CSP*, p. 336; *SP*, p. 170) is, in form and tone, somewhat similar to "Prime" and "Nones"; these three poems, describing the beginning, middle, and end of the day, form the series' foundation. The process of man emerging from the natural world and from the world of dreams, described in "Prime," is reversed in "Compline." Again, a series of "as" clauses slows the events, and the poem maintains a double focus of awareness and experience. But, because of what "happened" in "Nones," no general myth can cover the movement, as it does in "Prime"; as the body rejoins "plants in their chaster peace" there

>   . . . should come
>   The instant of recollection
>   When the whole thing makes sense: it comes, but all
>   I recall are doors banging,
>   Two housewives scolding, an old man gobbling,
>   A child's wild look of envy,
>   Actions, words, that could fit any tale,
>   And I fail to see either plot

---

from Alexandria visiting an intellectual friend. We are walking along, engaged in philosophical argument. Our path takes us past the base of Golgotha. Looking up, we see an all too familiar sight—three crosses surrounded by a jeering crowd. Frowning with prim distaste, I say, 'It's disgusting the way the mob enjoy such things. Why can't the authorities execute criminals humanely and in private by giving them hemlock to drink, as they did with Socrates?' Then, averting my eyes from the disagreeable spectacle, I resume our fascinating discussion about the nature of the True, the Good, and the Beautiful" (pp. 168–169). This fancy seems exactly what is dramatized in "Vespers": an intellectual discussion in the foreground, with a *paysage moralisé* of the Crucifixion in the background, as a means of indicating that the fact about mankind represented by the Crucifixion is always present, in the background but visible, either to be ignored or taken account of.

> Or meaning; I cannot remember
>> A thing between noon and three.
>>>>> [*CSP*, p. 336; *SP*, pp. 170–171]

The poem is full of puns, off-rhymes, half-significances because the experience dramatized does not compose itself into
a plot with a meaning. Not that the poem is formless; Auden
uses form to place man between the "chaster" world of
plants, which the body can join, and the as yet unplotted,
uninterpreted, raw experience, which the self has journeyed
into. The poem contrasts the regular systems of the universe
and of the body, which "talk a language of motion / I can
measure but not read," and the irregular system of dreams
with

> . . . its unwashed tribes of wishes
>> Who have no dances and no jokes
> But a magic cult to propitiate
>> What happens from noon till three,
> Odd rites which they hide from me.
>>>>> [*CSP*, pp. 336–337; *SP*, p. 171]

At this exact moment the series takes a turn. What happens
between noon and three will be propitiated, but by the odd
and unspectacular rites of dreams. Immediately before this,
in the second stanza of "Compline," the speaker has defined
and accepted his uniqueness as a conscious self existing between the motions and rhythms of both universe and body:

> But, knowing I neither know what they know
>> Nor what I ought to know, scorning
> All vain fornications of fancy,
>> Now let me, blessing them both
> For the sweetness of their cassations,
>> Accept our separations.   [*CSP*, p. 336; *SP*, p. 171]

his statement is consistent with the picture of man that
merges in "Prime," where man "falls" into history and
ence into multiplicity and a unity that can only be de-
:ribed in terms of paradox and tension. The poet prays for
ie ability to bless man's multiplicity: clearly, the primary
ibject is the nature of man, not the requiredness of a re-
gious description of his existence. Rather than seeking an
nage of fusion of the disparate parts, the speaker, forsaking
ill vain fornications of fancy," turns toward an understated,
napocalyptic vision of man's place in the world:

> Can poets (can men in television)
>   Be saved? It is not easy
> To believe in unknowable justice
>   Or pray in the name of a love
> Whose name one's forgotten: . . .
> That we, too, may come to the picnic
>   With nothing to hide, join the dance
> As it moves in perichoresis,
>   Turns about the abiding tree.   [*CSP*, p. 337; *SP*, p. 172]

istead of the prophetic mode, the sequence here moves to
complex, often moving, ultimately, I think, sublime mode
imposed playfully of bits and oddments of vocabulary and
:ference.

This last stanza illustrates the strategy of the whole series,
ie union of mixed strands of language into a flowing and
umane but self-deprecating voice that is at once detached
id involved, conversational and reflective, fanciful and
irnest. The image of the rending of the veil is crucial: as an
nage of the dissolution of the classical distinction between
ie traditionally sacred and the traditionally profane, it sanc-
ons a mode of secular, profane art. At the precise moment
f the tragedy of the Crucifixion, events occur that both re-

veal to man his fallen nature and suggest that its redemption lies not in escape or denial but in recognition of the openness of history and self. Thus the Crucifixion, like the Incarnation in *For the Time Being*, the Fall in *Bucolics*, and Pentecost in the great odes on that subject, is presented as a humanizing event.

"Compline," although it is the liturgical completion of the day, is followed by "Lauds" (*CSP*, p. 337; *SP*, p. 172), both a morning prayer and the last prayer of the night vigil. Its double status suggests the resumption of the cycle completed by "Compline." Though formally intricate, the poem itself presents fewer problems than does the question of its place in the whole: how to view its cyclical form in the linear structure of the series. It is in the form of the medieval Spanish *cossante*, a simple yet highly artificial, and, in its interweaving of repeated lines, ritualistic form. As such, it sharply modulates the meditative, personal tone of "Compline." The shift is, in fact, so radical that it is difficult to agree with Spears that "the concern is no longer with individual guilt, but with others: communion is restored." [12] If this were so, it would seem to have the effect of negating everything the series has said about the difficulty of attaining the "communion"; the insistent argument of the series is that there *is* no easy way of communion, that no retreat into ritual *per se* will provide refuge, that it is even a potentially dangerous procedure because it is likely to be merely an escape. At the opposite end of the spectrum is Adams' view that Auden is "playing with perspective for its own sake," that he is throwing one radically divergent kind of material against another for effect only. "Lauds" does create a wrenching of tone and perspective, one that must be accounted for.

12. *Auden*, pp. 320–321.

The placement of the earliest morning poem at the end of the cycle also needs to be explained. One might argue that Auden is asserting by this means the continuity of the cycle and, indeed, its cyclicality. But if this is his aim, he has chosen an odd way of achieving it, for even if the nature of a cycle is such that we ought to be able to break into it at any point, to rearrange this particular cycle seems more a qualification than an endorsement of it, an attempt to make us view it not in terms of ritualistic piety but to view the pietistic simplicity of the ritual in the light of all that has "happened" in the less ritualistic parts of the cycle.

This seems to me exactly what Auden is doing: defining carefully both the value and the limits of ritual, not as a way of life nor as a substitute for involvement in the "ethically serious" secular world, but rather as a demonstration, highly artificial, of the order that could and should but does not exist in the fallen world of history. Auden dangles, as it were, this purest and most cyclical poem at the end of the series to demonstrate the chasm between its formal, artistic harmony and the cacophony of existence. The juxtaposition completes his diagram of possible modes of existence and of the chasm in which man, trying to act in the fullest sense of the term, exists.

The movement and pattern of "Lauds" dominate its statement. It seems to have no direct reference to the events of the other poems, either to the experience, the cryptically hinted "story," or to the events of the Passion implicit in the total pattern. In its simplicity of statement and elaborateness of design, however, it performs several crucial functions.

More than anything else, it asserts that the cycle it completes is worth beginning again. Its lightness and simplicity does not contradict the foregoing poems, but it suggests what is implicit in even the darkest of them, "Nones," that the fallen world is redeemable, that the process of acting and falling and hence engaging in a kind of Crucifixion is worth repeating. It does so simply by praising "this green world temporal," the world in which we live, and by implying that all that inevitably follows from engagement in the world of experience, of history, can be celebrated in the simple, festival terms of the song.

It also refocuses attention on the question of kinds of form and order. It is another instance of a verbal plurality that is part of the larger plurality of the whole sequence. By being cyclical in its form, by both ending and beginning larger cycles (of the day, of the canonical hours), by using such images as the mill-wheel, and by celebrating the temporal world, it rekindles interest in what is perhaps the dominant assertion of the series. Man exists in worlds of both cyclical and linear time. He lives at once in the real world of natural events, which operate cyclically, according to laws of repetition, and in a real world of historical events, which progress in a linear fashion, noniteratively. This is perhaps the most important instance of man's double, medial position. As a biological creature he exists in patterned time. As a fallen, evolved, creature, he lives in open, kairotic time, in which he has choice and, however misused it is likely to be, freedom, part of which is the freedom to try to redeem time.

But no moral does justice to the whole artifice, which is one of Auden's masterpieces. It is more than a complex pattern of intricate patterns, and the final poem, simultaneously simple and complex almost beyond description, is a reading guide to the whole, which succeeds in the highest aim of locational art: to define man without limiting him. Its verbal action, complex and lacking plot, is to suggest the conditions

in which action in the fullest sense of transforming phenomenal and psychological reality into actuality can occur. This
in turn becomes the central subject of Auden's next great
serial work, *Thanksgiving for a Habitat*.

6. *An Architecture of Humanism*

Action, approached tentatively in *Horae Canonicae*, re
ceives positive and extensive consideration in *Thanksgiving*
for a Habitat. The series explores two kinds of action, artistic
making and human speech, constructing an elaborate archi
tectural metaphor for both, and for the interaction of the
two. More teasingly audacious in manner than either *Bucolic*
or *Horae Canonicae,* it pulls together the various threads that
run through Auden's later poetry.

The series is based on a view of the nature of man's exis
tence in the world, of which the poems and the house are
diagrammatic examples and which the poems, individually
and as parts of a whole, explain. That man can both work and
play, that he is both *homo faber* and *homo ludens,* is ulti
mately cause for thanksgiving, and the poems celebrate the
fullness and variety of man's position as a complex, limited
temporal being.

We read the poems as if we were taking a guided tour of
the house, seeing the life that is lived there and the ways the
life and the building complement and define each other. More
than any other work of Auden's, the sequence focuses on
man's way of locating himself by fabricating a humane habi
tat as an example of making a "second nature," a fit place for
man, both as a creature and as a unique being. It celebrates

homo faber in two senses—man as the only architectural species and the poet as verbal architect—and thus invites continual comparisons among the described house, the poetic edifice that describes it, and the acts of making and self-disclosure that occur within the house. It also honors the range of activities and relationships that occur within the house: eating, sleeping, excreting, bathing, cooking, talking; I-it, I-you, I-me, and I-thou. The journey through the house is taken at a slow, almost processional pace: the particularity of each ceremony of living, from bath-taking to poetry-making to dining to sleeping, is honored, both for itself and for its participation in a well-built fabric.

The sequence is also a historical document which focuses on the present but ranges wide in its allusions and suggests by them comparisons between this age and others. The casual, playful manner makes a major statement about our time: our architecture, our poetry, our public space, are, as Auden puts it elsewhere, no longer on the grand scale:

The personal excellence left for the poet's praise is today largely confined to private life. The hero in modern poetry is generally not someone who wields power for the general good but someone who, by resisting the pressure of impersonal powers, preserves his integrity and remains himself.[1]

Humanism, as Geoffrey Scott says, "has two enemies—chaos and inhuman order," [2] and it will oppose them in different ways and degrees according to which at a given moment is the greater threat. To Auden the primary enemy today is inhuman order, the attempts made by "impersonal powers"

1. "The Dyer's Hand: Poetry and the Poetic Process," *Anchor Review*, II (1957), 291.
2. *The Architecture of Humanism: A Study in the History of Taste*, 2d ed. (Garden City: Doubleday, n.d.), p. 181.

to reduce men to faceless numbers. The poet carries the banner of humanity, reminding the authorities that he is *homo ludens* and *homo faber;* he plays, thus "mak[ing] nonsense of any doctrine of historical necessity"; he fashions well, creating a place in which, because it is built to human scale, he may act as a unique being.

Our sense of both *homo faber* and *homo ludens* comes from the ambling catholicity of the poems that forces us to stumble across points of importance, from the playfully but pointedly intricate surfaces of the poems, from our overall sense of a well-made structure. We have a simultaneous sense of largeness and smallness about both the house and the poetic construct. It is larger than we expect a simple country house to be, and just the right size for the life lived there. Still, it is lamentable that our fabricated world, the human artifice thought of in general terms, should have shrunk to this size, yet there is a warning to the authorities that the party of humanity, scattered across the earth, its public forums reduced and domesticated, retains life and spirit, embodied in its good-humored resolve: "I have no gun, but I can spit."

The core of the sequence is the continually revised and restated set of correspondences among the house, the poems, and the quality of life; all three continually serve as tropes for each other. They embody a spirit very close to that which Scott, discussing Renaissance architecture, describes:

This principle of humanism explains our pleasure in Renaissance building. . . . It forms the common tie between the different phases—at first so contradictory—of Renaissance style. It accounts for its strange attitude, at once obsequious and unruly, to the architecture of antiquity. It explains how Renaissance architecture is allied to the whole tendency of thought with which it was contemporary—the humanist attitude to literature and life.

Man, as the savage first conceived him, man, as the mind of

science still affirms, is not the centre of the world he lives in, but merely one of her myriad products, more conscious than the rest and more perplexed. A stranger on the indifferent earth, he adapts himself slowly and painfully to inhuman nature, and at moments, not without peril, compels inhuman nature to his need. A spectacle surrounds him—sometimes splendid, often morose, uncouth and formidable. He may cower before it like the savage, study it impartially for what it is, like the man of science; it remains, in the end, as in the beginning, something alien and inhuman, often destructive of his hopes. But a third way is open. He may construct, within the world as it is, a pattern of the world as he would have it. This is the way of humanism, in philosophy, in life, and in the arts.[3]

This accurately summarizes the status of architecture in the sequence. Its details, interesting and complex in their own right, are related by the governing architectural figure to Auden's central moral and philosophical suppositions: they constitute an elaborate architectural demonstration of fundamental moral axioms about man's place and his nature.

The axioms are, in fact, stated in axiomatic terms in Auden's review of Hannah Arendt's *The Human Condition*, a book of which he says:

Every now and then, I come across a book which gives me the impression of having been especially written for me. . . . In the case of a "think" book, it seems to answer precisely those questions which I have been putting to myself. . . . Miss Hannah Arendt's *The Human Condition* belongs to this small and select class.[4]

Auden views the book as "an essay in Etymology, a re-examination of what we think we mean, what we actually mean and what we ought to mean" when we use certain

3. *Architecture of Humanism*, pp. 178–179.
4. "Thinking What We Are Doing," *Encounter*, 12 (1959), 72.

pivotal terms; hence he reviews it by presenting some of its definitions as if it were a dictionary. The definitions constitute a succinct and accurate glossary to Auden's mature poetry, and they deserve close attention.

Insofar as man is a part of nature, "a biological organism subject like all other creatures" to "the temporal cycle of generation," his primary form of activity is "*labour*, any behaviour which is imposed by the need to survive." As a laboring animal, he

does not act; he exhibits human behaviour, the goal of which is not a matter of personal decision, but dictated by the natural instinct to survive and propagate life. . . . Though he is social, [his experiences] are essentially *private* and subjective. . . . He needs the presence of his fellows not as persons but as bodies, another set of muscles, a fertile member of the opposite sex.

[pp. 72–73; Auden's italics]

Man, unlike other animals, is also "a mortal individual," aware of his mortality. At the same time, he is aware that in the realm of nature there are, besides other mortal beings, permanent things: "the earth, the ocean, the sun, moon, and stars, which are always there."

Out of this double awareness, of human mortality and the everlastingness of things, arises the desire and hope of transcending the cycle of natural birth and death by *making a world* of things which endure and in which, therefore, man can always be at home. . . . Man the maker is not social, that is, for the process of fabrication he requires the presence, not of human beings, but of the various materials out of which he fashions a world.

[p. 73; Auden's italics]

The things he makes, however, require "a human community" to use them; and "the fabricated world has an objective reality which is lacking in both human behaviour and human action."

Besides being a member of a species of creatures and a mortal individual who can make immortal objects, "every man is a unique person . . . the like of whom never existed before and will never exist again." "*Action*" is unique to each person and is a means of disclosing that uniqueness: "only the person requires a *public* realm of other persons to whom through his *actions* he discloses who he is. For human action is unintelligible without speech whereby the agent identifies who he is, what he is doing, and what he intends to do" (pp. 73–74; Auden's italics). In the modern age, however, there has been a reversal and a confusion of these spheres and activities:

> Public life, in the Greek sense, has been replaced by social life, that is to say, the private activity of earning one's bread is now carried on in public.
>
> What a modern man thinks of as the realm where he is free to be himself and to disclose himself to others, is what he calls his private or personal life, that is to say, the nearest modern equivalent to the public realm of the Greeks is the intimate realm.
>
> [p. 76]

Besides the partial reversal of the public and the private, there has also been in the modern age a diminution of our sense of the world: "World alienation," as Miss Arendt points out, "and not self-alienation, as Marx thought, has been the hallmark of the modern age." This, she argues elsewhere, is at least in part the result of "a two-fold flight from earth into the universe and from the world into the self." [5]

The sequence is not just about a house, although the actual

5. *Human Condition*, pp. 231, 7.

constructions, both the poetic and the architectural ones, are of great importance. Both have a multiple status: they are instances of the "intimate realm," which is to say of the arena of significant action; they are diagrams of all the facets of man mentioned; and they are fabricated objects, instances of the well-made and well-spoken.

"Prologue: The Birth of Architecture" (*ATH*, p. 3; *SP*, p. 181), the first poem of the series, opens with a complicated play of words that carefully defines a temporal perspective:

> From gallery-grave and the hunt of a wren-king
>   to Low Mass and trailer camp
> is hardly a tick by the carbon clock, but I
>   don't count that way nor do you:
> already it is millions of heartbeats ago
>   back to the Bicycle Age,
> before which is no *After* for me to measure,
>   just a still prehistoric *Once*.
>
> [*ATH*, p. 3; *SP*, pp. 181–182]

These lines map a medial position for "you" and "me," the speaker and the reader, that corresponds to the way in which we actually measure time. Miss Arendt says:

Seen from the viewpoint of man, who always lives in the interval between past and future, time is not a continuum, a flow of uninterrupted succession; it is broken in the middle, at the point where "he" stands; and "his" standpoint is not the present as we usually understand it but rather a gap in time which "his" constant fighting, "his" making a stand against past and future, keeps in existence.[6]

Auden crystalizes this gap between past and future in his tone—"I / don't count that way nor do you"—and in the jumbling of historical instances of architecture. Each repre-

6. *Between Past and Future: Six Exercises in Political Thought* (New York: Meridian, 1963), p. 11.

sents its age, but from the point of view of the present "gap in time," all are the work of "the same Old Man," the proto-typical architect. From the viewpoint of the present, all build-ings simply belong to the past; since each expresses the "pres-ent" at which it was built, we cannot really distinguish among them, not knowing any past moment as a present moment. As the scrambled listing indicates, each point in the past is, from the viewpoint of the present, cotemporal with every other. The argument, simple perhaps in its logic, but teasing in its implications, is buttressed by a subtly counterpointed rhythm, which helps to sharpen our awareness of the con-nection between time-sense and making.

The second part of the poem contrasts history—by which Auden really means not the past but the present—and nature:

> No world
> wears as well as it should but, mortal or not,
>   a world has still to be built
> because of what we can see from our windows,
>   that Immortal Commonwealth
> which is there regardless: It's in perfect taste
>   and it's never boring but
> it won't quite do. Among its populations
>   are masons and carpenters
> who build the most exquisite shelters and safes,
>   but no architects, any more
> than there are heretics or bounders: to take
>   umbrage at death, to construct
> a second nature of tomb and temple, lives
>   must know the meaning of *If*.
>
> [*ATH*, pp. 3–4; *SP*, p. 182]

The world of nature is "regardless": it is there on a noncon-tingent basis, and it is incapable of "regarding," either itself or anything else. In contrast, man, because he knows the

meaning of "if," because he lives in freedom as well as necessity, must construct a "second nature," one that expresses his
own awareness of his mortality. Hence architecture, unlike
carpentry or masonry, becomes a defining human act that
proceeds not from skill but from man's sense of his own
mortality. The play of language, rhythms, and logic is cease-
less, but it is difficult to find the exact word for the tone, at
once restless and grave, witty and earnest. "A world has still
to be built" despite our knowing that it won't "wear well,"
but also, has yet to be built—and the explanation, isolated in
a line, is "because of what we can see from our windows,"
because the world of nature "won't quite do." This illogic
makes sense: we must *make* a *world* because the realm of
nature is immortal. "Our windows" are our senses, and the
phrase pinpoints what it is that makes building a world necessary: we are separated from the realm of nature by—to use
the necessary tautology—our sense of separateness from it; it
is immortal (does not know it will die, lasts forever, differs
from the realm of man), and we are not. Thus our architecture ("tomb and temple") at once expresses and partially
transcends our sense of our mortality.

The title of the series and of the second poem, "Thanksgiving for a Habitat" (*ATH*, p. 5; *SP*, p. 183), suggests a familiar paradox: habitat is a biological term, and points to architecture as a natural and biological mode of expression.
Each species has its appropriate habitat, and so does man;
man, however, creates a habitat of his own that expresses his
awareness of his uniqueness in the natural order:

> Still, Hetty Pegler's Tump
> is worth a visit, so is Schönbrunn,

> to look at someone's idea of the body
> that should have been his, as the flesh

Mum formulated shouldn't: that whatever
  he does or feels in the mood for,

stocktaking, horseplay, worship, making love,
  he stays the same shape, disgraces
a Royal I.   [*ATH*, p. 5; *SP*, p. 183]

Auden treats man as a species to be classified; the precise
feature that identifies man is that man is not simply a creature
but also an individual, hence unclassifiable. He is a "Royal I,"
an ego that experiences itself as sovereign, as supranatural:

  We know all about graphs
and Darwin, enormous rooms no longer
  superhumanize, but earnest

city planners are mistaken: a pen
  for a rational animal
is no fitting habitat for Adam's
  sovereign clone.   [*ATH*, p. 6; *SP*, p. 184]

Clone is an interesting term. Auden uses a biological term to
describe that in man which distinguishes him from the order
of nature and a plural term that means "genetically identical"
to describe man's uniqueness and singularity. Clone is the
aggregate of organisms descended asexually from a single
common ancestor; man experiences himself as sovereign,
"a Royal I," whose being is the result of asexual reproduction.
As so often, Auden's comically mixed diction is the direct
result of his use of terms to define man as a being both natural
and supranatural. The play of language—pen, rational, animal,
habitat, sovereign, clone—maps the field in which man exists.
  Even more elaborately than "The Birth of Architecture,"
this poem plays with perspective as a means of defining the
human position:

        I ought
    to outlast the limber dragonflies

as the muscle-bound firs are certainly
    going to outlast me: I shall not end
down any esophagus, though I may succumb
    to a filter-passing predator,

shall, anyhow, stop eating, surrender my smidge
    of nitrogen to the World Fund
with a drawn-out *Oh* (unless at the nod
    of some jittery commander

I be translated in a nano-second
    to a c.c. of poisonous nothing
in a giga-death).   [*ATH*, p. 7; *SP*, pp. 184–185]

The witty perambulation defines man's place between nano-seconds and giga-death, trees and dragonflies, devouring "filter-passing predators" that can destroy man and larger esophaguses that cannot. To deal with the points as simple oppositions, however, reduces to a mechanical opposition a very intricate pattern, one like that on the other side of the looking glass, where things change shape and size and natural associations, but in a way that mirrors our actual existence. To read the poem properly, then, we must follow attentively the careful crosshatching of playful but pointed misassociation.

The basic patterns of the two sections of the first clause, defined by the stanza break, are, in skeletal form, parallel:

    I . . . outlast . . . dragonflies
    firs . . . outlast . . . me.

The movement of the first person pronoun from the nominative to the objective case places "me," so to speak, in between the small and the large, the animal and the vegetable, but when we add the modifiers, the reversals and shifts of perspective become much more complicated. The short-lived dragonflies sound both more vicious and more adaptable ("limber") than the long-lived firs; neither adjective, "limber" nor "muscle-bound," belongs to the order of the noun it modifies. "Ought to" is balanced by "are certainly going to," an antithesis that underscores the uncertainty of human life.

The basic terms of the next parallelism echo and compound those of the first: "I shall not end / down any esophagus"; "I may succumb / to a filter-passing predator." The last term is a kenning for a virus, and brings another multiple reversal: "succumb to a predator" suggests ending down an esophagus, not dying of a virus-induced disease. The constant shifts of size and scale in the two parallelisms create a constant play of shrinkage and enlargement that is almost Brobdingnagian. We might, for instance, associate dragonflies, predators, and firs with whatever might have a large enough esophagus to swallow a man, say a dragon; size, life span, and danger are woven into a texture of incomplete and incongruous associations, all aimed at a definition of man; statement and implication engage in continual mock warfare.

The pattern is repeated once again in the next stanza. To "stop eating, surrender my smidge / of nitrogen to the World Fund" rings several ironic chords with the preceding lines, making man both a predator and, dead, a very small mite of nitrogen in a very large World Fund. There is continual interaction among the various connotative luggage of each word, especially between the informal and scientific vocabularies. The parenthetical clause continues this, throwing "nod" and "jittery" against "nano-second," "c.c.," and "giga-death"; part of the point is the comic if unfunny handling of sophisticated weaponry by characters from opera buffa. A nano-second is a billionth of a second, a cubic centimeter of "poisonous nothing" is redundantly small (though that "poisonous nothing" is, presumably, radioactive debris, very potent "nothing"); a giga-death is what happens in a nuclear explosion—one death times a billion, occurring in one second divided into a billion. Things are becoming very large in scale, oddly small in terminology. "Giga" and "nano" suggest giant and nanny, the nursery and fairy tale as well as the laboratory and the battlefield, a set of correspondences that makes its own ironic point. The euphemism for death in this instance is "translated," and translated is exactly what is happening verbally: giga-death and nano-second are translations of "ordinary" words for death into terms at once mathematically precise, fanciful, and pertinent to the probable causes of death today. Within the whole series, large is getting larger and more vicious, and small is getting smaller, and the vocabulary is becoming more abstract. Nevertheless, the series of euphemisms for death reminds us that, in the end, dead is dead.

The play of usage and scale is preceded in "Thanksgiving for a Habitat" by a comparison between men and beasts:

> (I am glad
> the blackbird, for instance, cannot
>
> tell if I'm talking English, German or
>   just typewriting: that what he utters
> I may enjoy as an alien rigmarole.)

[*ATH*, pp. 6–7; *SP*, p. 184]

Rigmarole is both funny and precise, and doubly distinguishes man and animals. Animals are not capable of speech ("tell" here has a double sense, "know" and "speak")—which makes them comfortable to be around—and particularly not capable of translation. Translation for Auden is an intensely human and even religious act ("the Pentecostal marvel") and refers not only to translingual exchange but also to the kind of word play that goes on incessantly in this poem.

Immediately following the passage concerning kinds of death is another, less sanguine, comparison of man and animal. "Should conventional / blunderbuss war"

> invest my bailiwick, I shall of course
>   assume the submissive posture:
> but men are not wolves and it probably
>   won't help.   [*ATH*, p. 7; *SP*, p. 185]

That men are not wolves is, in this instance, not to man's credit: a wolf will not attack someone in the "submissive posture," as men will. Metaphorically, then, men *are* wolves. The same point is made by the double meaning of "conventional war," for war is "conventional" only among men. Hence, a whole series of comparisons of size and language is framed by a definition of man in comparison to other animals that has positive and negative aspects. The elaborate system of antitheses and comparisons is part of the complex enterprise of defining man's position and nature. To reduce him to a simple Linnaean oxymoron like "rational animal" is to ignore the richness of his existence and to suggest as a habitat for him nothing more "fit" than a city planner's logical pen.

The poem ends, appropriately, with a biological definition of man's only partially biological status:

> Territory, status,

> and love, sing all the birds, are what matter:
>   what I dared not hope or fight for
> is, in my fifties, mine, a toft-and-croft
>   where I needn't, ever, be at home *to*

> those I am not at home *with*, not a cradle,
>   a magic Eden without clocks,
> and not a windowless grave, but a place
>   I may go both in and out of.   [*ATH*, p. 7; *SP.*, p. 185]

Again man is in-between. The simple definition of the home, a place that, unlike cradle and grave, can be gotten out of and gone into, expresses the relation of architecture to human mortality. This is coordinated with the "hominess"—"toft-and-croft"—of the language: style becomes a second image of the architecture.

"Thanksgiving for a Habitat" prepares us for the tour that follows, but the first room visited, "The Cave of Making" (*ATH*, p. 8; *SP*, p. 186), the workroom reached only by an outside stairway, adds a new dimension by making explicit and extended the comparison between poetry and architecture; the title itself, by defining poetry as making, helps to indicate the parallel. The poem is also an elegy to Louis Mac-Neice, albeit an unconventional one:

> . . . dear Shade, for your elegy
>   I should have been able to manage
> something more like you than this egocentric monologue,
>   but accept it for friendship's sake.
>
> $\qquad\qquad\qquad\qquad$ [*ATH*, p. 11; *SP*, p. 189]

Like most elegies, it raises questions about death, and like most elegies for poets, it raises questions about the nature of poetry. The connection between awareness of mortality and poetic making is particularly important in this sequence, which emphasizes a point made in the review of Arendt's *The Human Condition*. Auden quotes a crucial passage from the book:

"Birth and death presuppose a world which is not in constant movement, but where durability and relative permanence make appearance and disappearance possible, which existed before any one individual appeared in it and will survive his eventual departure. Without a world into which men are born and from which they die, there would be nothing but everlasting recurrence, and deathless everlastingness of the human as of any other species." [7]

This passage helps to indicate why Auden so emphasizes poetry as an act of making (as opposed, in particular, to expressing or convincing), why he so lauds such makers as Weland and Hephaestos, both of them smiths, artisan artists, workers in permanent metals. "The Cave of Making" keeps us continually poised between awareness of the dead friend and the live maker, then, to suggest the integral connection between awareness of mortality and artistic making; this connection is what the poem is fundamentally about. If poetic making is a kind of architecture, then the reverse is true, and the poem underscores the notion that any and all acts of making a world are tinged with awareness of mortality. The sentiment is not a simple *ars longa* notion. We make a world because we feel our own mortality in comparison to the everlastingness of things, but not to escape from this awareness; on the contrary, as the passage Auden quotes from *The Human Condition* indicates, we do so in order to create a place in which, as unique persons, we may live. Hence the poet is happy to have the shade of his friend with him "until cocktail time," that is, until he is through with his tasks of making and can proceed to the world of the living.

The experience of reading the poem, stately but neither funereal nor solemn in its movement, is one of seeing the details, the trivia which are its raw materials, achieve the status of well-made art: "silence / is turned into objects." It develops parallel contrasts between the enclosure and the livelier, noisier world around it and between the objects and

7. *Encounter*, 12 (1959), 72.

the world from which they are made. When we come to the sections dealing specifically with Louis MacNeice, the contrasts are amplified, the life and the works of the maker put into continual juxtaposition.

The effect of "The Cave of Making" comes from combining the argument about art and mortality with the tone of familiar, but still elegiac, address to a dead friend. It moves from the living MacNeice to MacNeice dead but "present" in his art, to a general sense of death, from this to the act of making poetry and to its relation to life, and from this back to death in both particular and general. The movement seems ambling, but its fusing of the several themes is successful. By speaking continually to the subject of the elegy as if he were alive, and continually of his death, the living poet creates a sharp sense *of* his death, of the fact that his friend is not there, and of the connection between this awareness and the acts of making poetry. Architecture and verbal construct become so thoroughly mixed they cannot be separated. The words create a sense of the room, "an antre / more private than a bedroom even," in which they themselves are wrought into architectural objects, a room separate from "life" that, however, "saves" us from "deathless everlastingness," and hence becomes the absolutely right poem and room for entertaining thoughts, and the shade, of a dead friend.

The complex relations among words, sentences, lines, and stanzas also exist among the poems in the sequence. The next two poems, "Down There," and "Up There," establish a new architectural coordinate for the realms of nature and history. "Down There" (*ATH*, p. 14; *SP*, p. 189) is the past viewed in biological-evolutionary terms, the caves of primal man, his refuge from glaciation; it is also the "safe anchor" of civil life. "Up There" (*ATH*, p. 15; *SP*, p. 190) is the storehouse of useless oddments of the historical past. The two co-ordinated poems recall Auden's favorite quotation from Whitehead: civilization is a precarious balance of trivial order and barbaric vagueness. The house is the image of civilization, and here, as elsewhere in the series, Auden carefully defines the triviality and the vagueness as a way of approaching what precariously exists at their intersection.

If the sequence is based in part on the relationship of man's status as a mortal individual and a unique person to his status as a biological organism, it is quite appropriate that the central poems deal with the self-preserving natural functions of biological organisms, with plumbing and food, bathroom and kitchen. The first, "The Geography of the House" (*ATH*, p. 16; *SP*, p. 191), is a witty scatological lyric that, being in a different mode and eliciting a new response from the reader, makes its point that man is a biological organism:

> Lifted off the potty,
> Infants from their mothers
> Hear their first impartial
> Words of worldly praise:
> Hence, to start the morning
> With a satisfactory
> Dump is a good omen
> All our adult days.   [*ATH*, p. 16; *SP*, p. 192]

The major themes of the sequence make a comic appearance here: "All the Arts derive from / This ur-act of making." The mode necessarily makes comment sound pompous, but this in itself is important: if we are to acknowledge man's whole complex existence, we must acknowledge biological necessity, and not just as an abstraction.

Human beings are natural creatures, they do excrete, and the nervous giggle the poem at first produces testifies to our unsettled feelings about the subject. Auden is aware of Freud, Swift, Erik Erikson, and Norman O. Brown: there are those who indeed take the view that this ur-act of making is the basis of art, and the poem has a serious point to make about the theories. To confuse the origin with the result would be a dangerous mistake, and the high spirits of the poem keep us from it.

"Encomium Balnei" and "Grub First, Then Ethics" are both witty elaborations and explanations of the notion that "the nearest modern equivalent to the public realm of the Greeks is the intimate realm." The former announces its form:

> what Eden is there for the lapsed
> but hot water
> snug in its caul
> widows
> orphans
> exiles may feel as self-important
> as an only child
> and a sage
> be silly without shame
> present a Lieder Abend
> to a captive audience of his toes
> retreat from rhyme and reason into some mallarmesque
> syllabic fog
> for half an hour.   [*ATH*, p. 21; *SP*, p. 196]

The poem is indeed a mallarmesque syllabic fog, without punctuation or rhyme or regular line length; it has much in common, not formally but in general argument, with "In Praise of Limestone." The bath and the irregular form are both escapes from the well-formed and regular world, escapes that make us feel that both the "Pilgrim's Way" and the

"War Path" have been transformed into "a square in the Holy City," that civility is possible. The visual arrangement of phrases and clauses on the page is a diagram of the syntactical arrangements, and allows both for the kind of positional humor so familiar in Auden and for the kind of associational logic that is represented by the healing properties of the bath. The ceremony of bath-taking is a saturnalian activity expressed in a saturnalian form.

There is also a running comparison, carried not only by direct allusion but also by play of diction, between the modern tub and the Roman bath. Even "if we no longer / go there to wrestle or gossip / or make love," and "if the tepidarium's / barrel vaulting has migrated / to churches and railroad stations," nonetheless

> to withdraw from the tribe at will
> > > be neither Parent
> > Spouse nor Guest
> > > is a sacrosanct
> political right.   [*ATH*, p. 21; *SP*, p. 195]

The resonances among poetic form and language, tone, mode of being, and architecture create a harmony, and, once again, if the theme is a modern shrinkage and reversal of our notion of the public, the poem itself carries out an enlargement that playfully counters that shrinkage.

The title of the eighth poem, "Grub First, Then Ethics" (*ATH*, p. 23; *SP*, p. 197), Auden's translation of Brecht's "*Erst kommt das Fressen, dann kommt die Moral*," seems at first to be flagrantly inappropriate; but the poem, in a rather meandering and tongue-in-cheek manner, finally arrives at a point at which the quasi-Marxist epigram has something very specific to do with the seemingly archcapitalistic bourgeois act of installing an American kitchen. In the process, the speaker draws a contrast, both linguistic and substantive, between our democratic and egalitarian age and the royal age of Mozart:

> Though built in Lower Austria,
>   do-it-yourself America
> prophetically blueprinted this
>   palace kitchen for kingdoms
> where royalty would be incognito.

[*ATH*, p. 23; *SP*, p. 198]

"Do-it-yourself America" planned the kitchen but did not build it; its blueprint, the emblem of mechanical efficiency, is prophetic, in the literal sense that the plan is a prophecy of the completed kitchen and in the metaphorical sense that the kitchen is a miracle. This is a "palace kitchen for kingdoms" in its elaborateness and in the sense, explained in the sixth stanza, that a home today is a kind of a kingdom, the modern substitute for "the public space." The whole elaborate and intentionally oversubtle discussion of the Age of Poise and its modern equivalents is a good example of the kind of fussy manner that gets Auden into trouble with critics who view style in less functional terms than he does. What Auden is doing is to treat modern manners as if they were the manners of the age of Beaumarchais. Since we make fewer distinctions between classes in terms of accent or dirty necks, since modern machines make all hands equally uncalloused, "the right note is harder / to hear." Nonetheless, the poem suggests, the distinctions are still made. Hence, the "fussy" surface and archly coy talk about Him and Her, being itself slightly out of tune, has a point to make by its inappropriateness.

The poem then proceeds to demonstrate ways in which "grub" precedes "ethics":

House-proud, deploring labor, extolling work,
    these engines politely insist
that banausics can be liberals,
    a cook a pure artist

    who moves everyman
    at a deeper level than
Mozart.   [*ATH*, p. 24; *SP*, p. 198]

The deeper level is, of course, the stomach, something that
Adam, Eve, the snake, Jew, and pigmy all have. The terms
labor and work are used with wit as well as philosophical
seriousness. The first line quoted, taken alone, suggests the
kitchen as a solution to the modern confusion between work
and labor. That the adjectives modify "engines" (a curious
term for kitchen appliances) is a way of surprising the reader,
with his view of the machine as the enemy of freedom. That
these engines "politely insist" continues the paradox: courtesy
does indeed seem to reign in the kitchen, carried out not by
men but by machines. "Banausics" are artisans, generally in a
pejorative sense; the term connotes a forge, and ties this cave
of making to such "antres" as "Weland's Stithy" ("The Cave
of Making," *ATH*, p. 8; *SP*, p. 186). Banausic refers both to
the servile class and to a pragmatic approach to things, and
fits nicely with the original sense of "liberal": "Original epithet of those 'arts' . . . that were 'worthy of free man': opposite to *servile* or *mechanical*" (*OED*). The dialectic of the
poem is latent in the diction: for a banausic to become a liberal by working in a pragmatic cave like a kitchen is for *labor*
to become *work*, feeding an art, and grub to lead to ethics.
Word play telescopes a tricky, sophisticated, and serious argument into a phrase; the liberation occurs in the words just
as it does in the kitchen.

The modern world generally lacks "public space," the arena of significant actions and speech by which, as Miss Arendt puts it, "men show who they are, reveal actively their unique personal identities and thus make their appearance in the human world," but which, "wherever people gather together . . . is potentially there." [8] The modern kitchen is a metaphor for the possibility of significant making in the modern age, which is in turn the prerequisite for speech and action, which are in turn the bases of the achievement of full humanity. The unexpectedness of the choice of the kitchen as metaphor, one more instance of the connection between verbal structure and architecture, is appropriate to the general strategy of the series.

In its last stanza, the poem turns, still maintaining the image of the transplanted kitchen, to the problem of "public space":

> The houses of our City
>   are real enough but they lie
> haphazardly scattered over the earth,
>   and her vagabond forum
> is any space where two of us happen to meet
>   who can spot a citizen
> without papers. So, too, can her foes. Where the
>   power lies remains to be seen,
> the force, though, is clearly with them: perhaps only
>   by falling can She become
> Her own vision, but we have sworn under four eyes
>   to keep Her up—all we ask for,
> should the night come when comets blaze and meres break,
>   is a good dinner, that we
> may march in high fettle, left foot first,
>   to hold her Thermopylae.
>
>   [*ATH*, pp. 25–26; *SP*, pp. 199–200]

8. *Human Condition*, pp. 159, 178.

"She," here, is the City as it is today, and the allusions to Greece call forth a comparison of our city, with its houses scattered haphazardly, to that of ancient Greece. We have no public forum in the architectural sense; but it exists, potentially, wherever citizenship, in the Roman or Greek sense, is recognizable without identity papers. When this happens, as it occasionally does, a forum is created. The foes of the city will recognize this encounter for what it is—highly subversive—and attempt to destroy it, but the party of humanity, through its comic subversions, will rally to its defense, a good dinner under its belt. Thus, in a sense different from that intended by Brecht but nonetheless important, the title once again applies.

Not only within this poem, but in the group of poems beginning with "The Geography of the House," a complex movement from the purely biological and private toward the public and historical occurs, a movement accomplished by means of multiple comic reversals. As this movement proceeds, we sense the slow and careful building of an edifice from the foundation upward. The last four poems move more clearly into that superficially private realm the series has been defining as "public." "For Friends Only" describes the guest room and the nature of friendship; "Tonight at Seven-Thirty" describes the dining room and draws a distinction between friendship and the public life; "The Cave of Nakedness" moves quickly back to the realm of the private and invites comparison not only with the realms described in the surrounding poems but also with that of "The Cave of Making"; and "The Common Life" describes the highest function of architecture as the creation of a space in which full humanity can be realized in an I-thou relationship.

"For Friends Only" (*ATH*, p. 27; *SP*, p. 200) is precise, simple, neither overly formal nor overly intimate, both invit-

ing and reticent; it defines with exactitude the tone of friendship and attempts to reproduce its language:

> Easy at first, the language of friendship
> Is, as we soon discover,
> Very difficult to speak well, a tongue
> With no cognates, no resemblance
> To the galimatias of nursery and bedroom,
> Court rhyme or shepherd's prose,
>
> And, unless often spoken, soon goes rusty.
>
> [*ATH*, p. 28; *SP*, p. 201]

As throughout the series, the form of address is a crucial
subject; here the form—based, as Fuller points out,[9] on word
count rather than syllable or accent count—makes its special,
low-keyed point: the language of friendship is unique, governed by a careful balance of familiarity and reserve. Fussy
attention is paid to what is beside the bed and what is and is
not proper behaviour, to distinctions between borrowing pa-
per and borrowing stamps. As the first "social" poem in the
series, its title has a double meaning: this room, this tone, this
code of behavior is reserved for friends; but there are limits
to friendship, and the room is for those who are only friends.

Its effect comes in part from the contrast of its simple directness with "Tonight at Seven-Thirty" (*ATH*, p. 29; *SP*, p.
202), which describes "the worldly rite" of a dinner in appropriately festive language. This is the most formally intricate of the poems, with elaborate stanzas, an elaborate
rhyme scheme and syllabic pattern, and an intricate play of
diction and reference. There is a shift in emphasis from the
preceding poems toward the way in which man fabricates
a social arrangement and attempts to achieve human commu-

9. *Reader's Guide*, p. 245.

nity. At the same time the inclusive form becomes a means of displaying an array of details that suggest the richness of the human position.

The poem opens with taxonomical and historical classifications of man in terms of his mealtime habits:

> The life of plants
> is one continuous solitary meal,
>   and ruminants
> hardly interrupt theirs to sleep or to mate, but most
>   predators feel
> ravenous most of the time and competitive
> always, bolting such morsels as they can contrive
> to snatch from the more terrified: pack-hunters do
>   dine *en famille*, it is true,
> with protocol and placement, but none of them play host
>   to a stranger whom they help first. Only man,
>   supererogatory beast,
>   Dame Kind's thoroughbred lunatic, can
>   do the honors of a feast.   [*ATH*, p. 29; *SP*, p. 202]

Besides being diagrammatic, the layering is festive, a playful design that mirrors the subject that its taxonomy defines. Man, the "supererogatory beast," can "do the honors of a feast," the form of eating that distinguishes him from other eaters. Formal design, social arrangement, and creaturely definition echo and instance each other. Arrangement, a kind of social fabrication, becomes a defining characteristic: the higher up the evolutionary ladder towards man we go, the more order becomes definitive and necessary. The poem itself becomes a festive arrangement:

> I see a table
> at which the youngest and oldest present
>   keep the eye grateful

> for what Nature's bounty and grace of Spirit can create:
>   for the ear's content
> one raconteur, one gnostic with amazing shop,
> both in a talkative mood but knowing when to stop,
> and one wide-traveled worlding to interject now and then
>   a sardonic comment, men
> and women who enjoy the cloop of corks, appreciate
>   depatical fare, yet can see in swallowing
>   a sign act of reverence,
>   in speech a work of re-presenting
>   the true olamic silence.   [*ATH*, p. 31; *SP*, p. 204]

The balance achieved formally and at the table are Calderesque: not just a series of equipoises but something like the ideal forum, the man-made object in which self-disclosure can occur. It is the meeting place of men and women, Nature and Spirit, young and old, speech and silence, reverence and digestion. The last stanza is one long declarative sentence that becomes processional, moving from the opening "I see a table" to the equally simple "true olamic silence." In between, the sentence expands, divides, reunites, poising the plain and the fancy, physical and spiritual, sensory and intellectual, noisy and conversational against one another in a grand concord that images a well-ordered but festival meal that is also food for a biological organism. Here, as in the series as a whole, the great triumph is the harmony of the mimetic, definitional, and festival offices of the poem, a harmony that is the basis of our sense of created human space.

The observation that much of the series is based on—that the modern world has reversed the traditional senses of public and private—is compounded by the next poem, "The Cave of Nakedness" (*ATH*, p. 32; *SP*, p. 204), a more "private," meditative, personal poem. Once again, poetic and architectural space reflect each other to define human space:

Bed-sitting-rooms
soon drive us crazy, a dormitory even sooner
    turns us to brutes: bona fide architects know
that doors are not emphatic enough, and interpose,
    as a march between two realms, so alien, so disjunct,
the no-man's-land of a stair. The switch from personage,
    with a state number, a first and family name,
to the naked Adam or Eve, and vice versa,
    should not be off-hand or abrupt: a stair retards it
to a solemn procession.   [*ATH*, p. 32; *SP*, p. 205]

The distance between private and public realms within the
private domain of the house is also the distance between man
the creature and man the conscious being. It also becomes
poetic distance, as the poem, in long lines, alternately twelve
and thirteen syllables, and compound, additive sentences, surveys the distance in various terms and gives a sense of that
"solemn procession." The poem develops this cave as an
image of both remembered womb—"Since my infantile entrance / at my mother's bidding into Edwardian England"
(*ATH*, p. 33; *SP*, p. 205)—and anticipated tomb—"when I
disband from the world"—that again reminds us of the carefully developed connection between making and mortality in
"The Cave of Making"; this, in effect, is the mirror image of
that poem. "The Cave of Nakedness" concentrates on aging,
the differences between youth and age, the sheer statistical
facts of mortal life—appropriately, since the aspect of man
represented by the bedroom, the person as a biological rather
than a social or individual being, is subject to biological laws
of repetition, growth, and decay.

The poles of "The Cave of Nakedness" are man as a "corporal contraption" and man as a "personage, / with a state
number, a first and family name"; the subject is the relation
between man viewed as an individual and man viewed as a

person, especially as these are manifested in different forms of speech. The journey to the bedroom is a beneficent vicarious reversion to the status of being an individual, created, as Auden says in "Words and the Word," "by sexual reproduction and social conditioning." As individuals, we exhibit "behaviour characteristic of the biological species and social group or groups to which we belong." As persons, we can "now and again, truthfully say *I*," and we can form communities: "we are uncountable, incomparable, irreplaceable." All consideration of human language, he continues, must recognize the differences between our use of words "as a code of communication between individuals and our use of them for personal speech" (*SW*, p. 120).

"The Cave of Nakedness" rests partly on a gentle irony arising from the use of very personal, chatty, idiosyncratic language to describe the area in which we are merely individuals, not persons, as if to illustrate that we are always both persons and individuals. The poem mocks the notion that the bedroom, whether used for lovemaking or sleeping (activities he suggests, without necessarily derogating either, which belong to the same category), is the arena of our greatest self-realization, and at the same time honors the activities of man as a "corporal contraption."

"The Cave of Nakedness" stands in contrast to "Tonight at Seven-Thirty" and also to "The Common Life" (*ATH*, p. 36; *SP*, p. 207), which describes the area in which truly personal speech can occur:

> A living room, the catholic area you
>   (Thou, rather) and I may enter
> without knocking, leave without a bow, confronts
>   each visitor with a style,

a secular faith. . . .

> There's no *We* at an instant,
>   only *Thou* and *I*, two regions
> of protestant being which nowhere overlap.
>
> [*ATH*, p. 36; *SP*, p. 207]

"The Common Life" has, perhaps, an anticlimactic effect that, far from being disappointing, is carefully keyed to the design of the whole, which demands at this point an instance of "personal speech." What we get is a fastidious, quiet poem about "conversational tics and larval habits," with an I-thou relationship imaged in such phrases as "were you to die, I should miss" your tics and habits. Precisely because it does not fulfill our preconceptions of personal speech, it is personal in a very exact way; its understatement is the signature of its honesty, which is the defining characteristic of personal speech. The whole series, in its many tones, represents a grand figure of personal speech; this poem is the part that most fully represents the whole.

The tonalities of the whole, in fact, are all instances of Auden's clearly articulated notion that our sense of humanness is at least as fully expressed in the playful as in the prophetic mode. The series, like much of Auden's poetry, is a tour de force: we can think of its own image—"that we / may march in high fettle, left foot first, / to hold her Thermopylae" (*ATH*, p. 26; *SP*, p. 200)—as a description of the tonal politics of the whole: its left-footed high fettle is its statement.

The series seems to me a substantial achievement partly because of the coherence of idea, art, organization, and tone, and partly because it answers questions with which Auden has been concerned since the very beginning of his long poetic career: What does it mean to act? What does it mean to say "I will"? What is the "I" and how can it act in the world?

Thanksgiving for a Habitat presents a philosophy of self and action that is ultimately anti-Marxist but is an answer to questions raised by Marxism. There are three kinds of human activity: laboring, making, and acting. Man is most fully human when he engages in all three, least human when he engages only in the first; and the crucial consideration is that the second is the necessary prelude to the third. The function of poetry in this formulation is at least dual: it is an act of making, part of the task of building the human artifice, "the second nature," in which man can act; it is also an instance of human disclosure, an instance of a very important, almost prototypical kind of acting. Full selfhood occurs in action properly understood and distinguished from behavior. Behaving, we act involuntarily as members of a species and a social or economic class, primarily concerned with maintaining and propagating the class and the species.

Auden is very much a partisan of humanity, one who believes that in our age the mere act of making and the maintenance of a personal voice are intensely, perhaps subversively, political acts. *Thanksgiving for a Habitat* is Auden's fullest expression of this point of view; once we accept the idea that by "intimate," in tone and dwelling, Auden means what "public" signifies in its classic use, the series makes a substantial political statement. The series is microcosmic and parabolic in a special way: it describes in miniature the "proper" relations among man's various activities, including his participation as an "actor" in larger groups; it locates the public realm, in its true, rather than its popular sense, as the sphere in which man may disclose his humanity;

and it instances a variety of actions of this sort. Its miniaturization is not, however, simply that of microcosm and parable; it is also a mimetic representation of the public realm in the modern world.

Auden attempts to represent the historical shift of the public realm into what was once considered the private, to represent the shrinkage of the sphere of significant action. Although he seems to espouse a kind of privatism and dissociation from the larger world, he is being primarily descriptive and analytical, not prescriptive; there is indeed a strain of sadness in the description. Nonetheless, granted the shrinkage of the public realm and the movement into the household of the activities once possible in polis and forum, the prescriptive and positive bent of the poem—recommending the creation of spheres of action wherever possible—remains dominant.

Auden's deepest concern is with the means of achieving humanity: not the place of the house in the large world but the occurrences within the house. The argument of the series puts its own language, its own architecture, in a special focus. If speech viewed as personal disclosure and not simply as communication is one of the definitional human acts, and if making, of which poetry is a prime example, is the precondition of significant human action, then the language of the poems has special exemplary functions: it instances human fabrication and disclosure. Auden takes the view that making language into speech and transforming words into verbal architecture are distinctive and estimable activities, and the language and craft of the poems become part of the definitional and celebratory purposes of the sequence. Poetry is analogous to other forms of disclosure and acts of making, to any other form of activity by which man expresses or achieves humanity; but it does not claim singularity. The poems are about themselves: this is a truism about modern poetry, but it has a special sense here. They are about themselves in that they build the architectural and philosophical space in which their language exists as significant speech; they make a true architecture of humanism.

Thanksgiving for a Habitat is an example of the transformation of the everyday world, the world that is at hand, into an authentic place where authentic deeds may occur. The poetry that describes this transformation may at first seem apolitical, or at least politically lethargic. Richard Ohmann, for example, in what can be taken as a fairly representative statement, argues that "the only 'political' question that remains alive for Auden" is "what kind of climate does society offer for the flourishing of art, and of the self?"

"Auden's apoliticalism," Ohmann continues, "can lead him to insensitivity," as in the claim that "the whole question of Communism, socialism, and capitalism is merely a 'party issue,' a debate over practical means . . . not a revolutionary issue which turns on differences in principle." To argue thus, says Ohmann, is "to ignore the heartbreaking human consequences of unregenerate capitalism . . . or of totalitarian Communism" and thus "to lose touch with feeling, as well as with social thought." [10]

What Ohmann and others who have either scorned or applauded Auden for his apoliticalism fail to see is that Auden's comments are part of a general commentary on the poverty of our notion of what politics is and on the failure of our age to recognize the fullest sense of action. It is worth looking at

10. Richard M. Ohmann, "Auden's Sacred Awe," in Spears, *Auden Essays*, p. 175.

the remarks Ohmann characterizes as intellectually and emotionally out of touch:

Today, there is only one genuine world-wide revolutionary issue, racial equality. The debate between capitalism, socialism and communism is really a party issue, because the goal which all seek is really the same . . . : to guarantee to every member of society, as a psychophysical organism, the right to physical and mental health. . . . What is peculiar and novel to our age is that the principal goal of politics in every advanced society is not, strictly speaking, a political one, that is to say, it is not concerned with human beings as persons and citizens but with human bodies, with the precultural, prepolitical human creature. It is, perhaps, inevitable that respect for the liberty of the individual should have so greatly diminished and the authoritarian powers of the State have so greatly increased from what they were fifty years ago, for the main political issue today is concerned not with human liberties but with human necessities.   [DH, p. 87]

Auden argues that our age has confused politics with house-keeping, with near disastrous consequences; it has got things backwards, making the state the guardian (granted, often a poor guardian) of our corporal well-being, and has created no space for acts and deeds, for self-disclosure and self-realization; it has thought of freedom in private, internal terms, not public terms of action. It has vastly reduced our freedom in the positive sense of that term: we cannot do as much as we once could. To be "political" in this popular context, then, means to become involved primarily in the tactics of labor, the means of serving the universally acceptable (if not accepted) goals of feeding the belly and warming the body: exemplary goals, but not political issues in the best sense. Hence, to write a poem celebrating a food stamp plan or a housing project—which would be, narrowly and popularly speaking, a political act—would not be "political" as Auden wants the term to be understood, and would in fact assist in the perpetuation of a false and in some ways inhuman view of politics. Conversely, to write a poem about making and acting would be prototypical political action, but not obviously so, and certainly not in the general sense of the term. To write a poem clarifying the use, abuse, and proper use of terms concerning politics, would, again, be an estimable political and poetic act. To compose, then, a series of poems that, among other things, discuss the relations of all of these matters—food and warmth, making and acting, speech and meaning—is both a major accomplishment and a political act of considerable substance.

Auden does not say that the miseries, horrors, and consequences of "unregenerate capitalism" and authoritarian Communism are matters to be ignored or countenanced; he says that the debates—and the wars—among proponents of various positions are not political in the fullest sense because the debates concern labor, not work, the individual, not the person. Auden's remarks try to clarify the issue and to put political debate into a humanistic context; he has not recommended that we ignore suffering or the ill consequences of party decisions. On the contrary, he has tried to establish a platform for the debate of political matters—properly understood—in language attentive to the entire range of human potentiality and need.

One cannot accept the rejoinder that Auden is merely stipulating definitions that allow him to avoid crucial issues, because the "semantic" issues Auden raises are substantive and argued with care. One of the conclusions toward which this study has pointed, in fact, is that, partly because of the care with which he raises "political" issues, Auden should properly be thought of as a profoundly political poet: he has addressed the questions of what being so in our age involves, and he has been endlessly inventive in finding verbal means by which to present and define his politics. He is not a pamphleteer, not a direct participant through his poetry in what he calls "party politics," but a man with a developing and intelligent political theory that he strives to embody in verbal artifices that themselves have political status, given a proper understanding of the term.

Thus we see an important step in a process that began early in Auden's career. *New Year Letter,* which was occasioned by political events, argues that the immediate crisis cannot be addressed without thinking about what it means to be human, what man's place in the world is; it is a defense of poetry as a means of answering questions of this order. It moves away from, but never really abandons the immediate questions of existence. It is not the beginning, but it is a signal event in a long and still continuing pilgrimage in search of truths about the human situation and of ways of using poetry to find them. Along the way, questions are asked, ceremonies are performed; the free trade zone between poetic making and humanist definition keeps enlarging; a world of style and meaning is built. The questions are of a piece: what kind of creature is man? what is the relation of his awareness of being in the world and his increasing knowledge of his physical-biological status as a creature? what is the nature of action? Always there is a skepticism about too final answers, too quick solutions: an awareness that a compass error in fundamental definition can lead, and in our time has led, to disasters. Always there is festival joy in the journey for its own sake.

The inclusive term for the questions and for the poetic exploration of them is humanism, a celebration of man and a refusal to look at any of his actions or products outside the context of the basic facts of his existence. The poet's pilgrimage becomes a part and a type of the larger journeys, the "immense journeys" of man evolving and man tracing his evolution:

> *We've covered ground since that awkward day*
> *When, thoughtlessly, a human mind*
> *Decided to leave the apes behind,*
> *Come pretty far, but who dare say*
> *If far be forward or astray,*
> *Or what we still might do in the way*
> *Of patient building, impatient crime,*
> *Given the sunlight, salt and time.*   [*ATH*, p. 39]

Every double-meaning phrase restates the certain uncertainty of the human position; the question asked—"who dare say"—is an honest one in both its meanings, in both its warning against daring to say too much and its candid puzzlement about our course. The conditions ("sunlight, salt and time") for continuation are "given"—have been granted and can be assumed; our skepticism and knowledge are the bases of, not escapes from, building well, acting, becoming fully human.

Index of Auden's Works

General Index

MAN'S PLACE

Designed by R. E. Rosenbaum.
Composed by Vail-Ballou Press, Inc.,
in 11 point linotype Janson, 3 points leaded,
with display lines in monotype Janson.
Printed letterpress from type by Vail-Ballou Press
on P & S offset, 60 pound basis.
Bound by Vail-Ballou Press
in Columbia book cloth
and stamped in All Purpose foil.